Small Quilts,
BIG Results

mini
master
pieces

LEARN HOW TO QUILT!
A Workbook of 12 Essential Blocks & Techniques

ALYCE BLYTH

Published in 2019
by Lucky Spool Media, LLC

www.luckyspool.com

5424 Sunol Blvd., Suite 10-118
Pleasanton, CA 94566

info@luckyspool.com

Text © Alyce Blyth
Editor: Susanne Woods
Designer: Page + Pixel
Illustrator: Kari Vojtechovsky
Photographer: Page + Pixel

Photographs on pages 13 and 44 by
Lehua Noel, photograph on pages 11 and
14 by Lauren Hunt, photographs on pages
16-17 by Amy Gibson

9 8 7 6 5 4 3 2 1
First Edition

Printed in China

Library of Congress Cataloging-in-
Publication Data available upon request

ISBN: 978-1940655390
LSID0048

contents

DEDICATION: *Jonathan and Isabelle – if I can do it, you can do it.*

Introduction

When I was trying to narrow down what would be the best concept to put forward for my first book, I should have known that it would be one with a little bit of everything and a whole lot of teaching.

From childhood, I have jumped from craft to craft and from project to project, constantly curious to learn and understand the processes involved. Woven throughout this was a determination to be a primary school teacher. As with my crafting, I dabbled with other career ideas throughout high school, but in the end, I graduated from university with a Bachelor of Education. However, life had other ideas. When my husband and I became parents soon after I finished university, I put teaching to the side for the time being.

It was when my son was just a few months old, that I discovered quilting through my local mums' group. A friend, with her mother, had made a quilt for her daughter and I was intrigued by the patchwork of cute fabrics – certainly nothing like the English paper pieced hexagon mini quilt I had seen my own mum make when I was a teenager. This looked much quicker to make and featured a lot more fabric! I began reading books and blogs on quilting. One day my husband bought me a little $200 sewing machine on sale! Along with it, he told me to stop reading and start sewing. So, really, that makes all of this his fault. Really.

I'm forever thankful that he did buy me that first machine. Soon after I started quilting, we moved to Japan for his work. The culture shock of living in a foreign country with two young children and transitioning from much family support to none, drove me deep into quilting during any spare time I could carve out. The incredible online quilting community there, became my guild, my sewing group, my quilting class and my main source of English-speaking friendship.

Whilst I have traded in my school teacher's registration for a sewing machine, the need to take what I have learned and share it has never left me. My biggest passion is encouraging and enabling the beginner quilter. Whether that beginner is brand new to patchwork or an established quilter tackling a new skill or technique for the first time, I love nothing more than to guide and support them step-by-step towards the goal of completing a quilt.

For four years, I achieved this via my blog, *Blossom Heart Quilts*. I quilted my way through our entire stay in Japan. I wrote tutorials, patterns and an eBook *(DIY Block Design)*. I also developed a reputation for making sampler quilts that explored a single quilting technique over the course of a year.

Once we moved back to our native Australia, I was able to transition that sharing into teaching in-person classes at a local quilt store, namely Amitie in Melbourne. When Amitie moved to a new location an hour and a half away, it was the incentive I needed to turn my attention back to writing a quilting book so that I could finally teach those beyond my post code.

Mini Masterpieces is the result. Included are twelve mini quilts that cover twelve different techniques, with a coordinating 6″ sampler block for each. Whether trying only a bite-sized sample of the technique or sinking your teeth in a little further and tackling a full mini quilt, the designs and projects I've included here are achievable for quilters of all skill levels.

The projects also pay homage to my deep love of color and fabric play. Woven throughout the quilt patterns are tips and tricks I've learned over the years to help you develop a stronger use of color and fabrics. Together we'll explore everything from rainbows and monochrome, to working with scraps and even some fussy cutting.

Mini Quilts + More

Why mini quilts? You can make minis with the goal of both learning and artistic expression; however, sometimes you may want a more practical reason for making them too. How do you use mini quilts anyway? I was once there, intrigued by the ease of them, but perplexed by what to do with them once they were finished. Too small for a baby quilt and there are only so many doll quilts my daughter can use!

But I realized that our side table needed a table runner or topper. An 18″ to 20″ square mini quilt top can easily become a pillow cover too (see page 17). And the most obvious use of all is to hang them on a wall (see page 16) to enjoy as the masterpieces they truly are. Whatever you decide, I'm excited to help you get started!

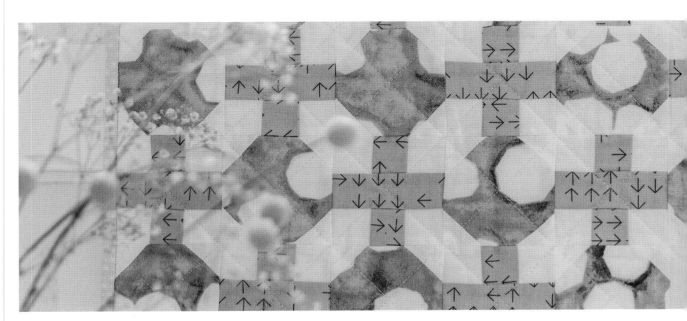

Getting Started

Welcome to mini mania! Making small modern quilts is something I'm crazy about and can't wait to share with you too. They are fun to display, not intimidating to try if you are new to quilting and perfect for swapping or gifting. *Mini Masterpieces* is a step-by-step, beginners-welcome guide to some essential patchwork techniques, organized into 12 easy-to-follow lessons to help you up your quilting game. Each lesson includes two small projects designed to help you celebrate one victory at a time as you master some new techniques. We'll start each lesson by making a manageable 6″ block to practice the focus technique as many times as it takes to get the hang of it. The second project is a multi-block mini quilt that allows you to create something more complex with your newly found sewing skills. At the back of the book, you'll find a handy glossary of all of the terms that are in **bold** throughout.

How to Use This Book

Start from the beginning and stitch your way through

This option is great for patchwork beginners or if a particular technique in the lesson is new to you. As we move through the book, we build on the skills learned in the prior lesson, progressively experimenting with and practicing a delightful variety of fundamental quilt making techniques.

A mini a month

With 12 mini quilts to make, you can make one a month for a whole year! There's no need to worry about whether it's January or not, just start working your way through the minis whenever you like. Completing one within a month can be easily achieved by cutting your fabrics one week, completing the top the next week, basting and beginning to quilt the following and finally finishing it all off in the final week. This option is a great way to create your own collection of home décor, or to build up a stash of handmade gifts as you progress.

Flip through and pick your favorites

Whether you are eager to dive in and begin tackling a new technique, or excited to make a particular quilt, picking and choosing which minis to make one at a time, is a totally valid way to sew your way through this book too. If you are looking to create a larger quilt (mini or otherwise), feel free to jump in and find a favorite block or two from the lessons.

The learning philosophy in my classroom is: 'make what you love'. Make this book work for you and your goals - use it to learn, to experiment, to challenge yourself, or to sew along with friends. Take your time and don't be afraid to abandon a practice block and try again. I know you'll end up making a mini masterpiece that you love and are proud to show off.

Tools and Techniques

Tools

Just like an artist has their palette of paint and jars of brushes, quilters too have a few essential bits and pieces they need to have on hand.

Sewing machine and feet

This is your most important tool. Spend some time getting to know your sewing machine by reading over the manual. This will help you understand how your particular machine works, introduce you to some of the common functions and parts, and describe what they do. A ¼″ foot that attaches to your machine is also useful, since this is a fairly standard **seam allowance**. Otherwise, use washi tape to mark the ¼″ seam line on your machine (see page 10). Another accessory that may be useful is a **walking foot** for quilting and binding.

8

Needles

Always keep an extra packet of machine needles on hand, as they can sometimes snap, or will eventually become blunt. Generally, it's a good idea to change the needle after every 8 - 10 hours of sewing (or after each big project). Be sure to check your sewing machine manual for how to change the needle and what type of needle the manufacturer recommends.

When hand sewing, selecting the right type and size of needle depends on what technique you are using. For this book, we will use milliners needles (also known as straw needles) for the appliqué lesson (see page 76). Needles have numbers that relate to their size. Confusingly, the larger the number, the smaller and finer the needle for the most part. For appliqué, I prefer a size 9 but experiment with a few to find your favorite.

Thread

Threads are made from a variety of fibers and are available in a selection of weights or thicknesses. Again, the higher the number, the finer the thread. I recommend buying a 50-weight cotton thread in an off-white or pale grey color to start with and this will cover all your needs — from piecing to the quilting. You may like to use a thicker thread like 40-weight for quilting by machine or a 12-weight if quilting by hand so that the stitches show up beautifully. I use Aurifil brand thread, as it's a strong, quality thread that doesn't break or shed a lot of fluff. But you might like to experiment to discover one that works best for you and your machine.

Rotary cutter + blades

Before the rotary cutter was invented in 1979, quilters had no choice but to cut their fabric by first marking out the required shapes and then cutting with scissors. While there is still a time and place for that method, there is no doubt that rotary cutting is more efficient and accurate. It looks a little like a pizza cutter and should be handled with care due to the extremely sharp blade. There are a few varieties, brands, sizes and colors to choose from. I recommend a rotary cutter with a 45mm size blade, an easy locking mechanism (because you should lock it every time you put it down to prevent injury to yourself and others who may accidentally come across it) and good protection around the blade when it is in the locked position. It may be a good idea to pick up a spare set of blades too, but they can be expensive. Try to gather these up when they are on sale or when you can use a store coupon. Save the plastic case in which the blades are sold in to safely store used blades too. Remember to mark the case with the word 'used' or 'old' so you know which are which. Rotary blades do get blunt with use, so remember to replace them when cutting the fabric gets that little bit more difficult.

Self-healing cutting mat

To use a rotary cutter, you need a craft mat to protect the surface underneath your fabric as you cut. These mats usually have a ruled grid on them to aid in cutting accurately. An 18″ × 24″ size mat is a great place to start.

Rulers

These are needed to provide a straight edge to cut against when you are rotary cutting. I recommend a 6½″ square ruler for cutting small pieces, a 6½″ × 12½″ for cutting larger pieces and a 6½″ × 24″ for cutting yardage. I prefer the Creative Grids brand of rulers as they have frosted edges to clearly show their markings.

Scissors

Even though we will do most of our cutting with rotary cutters, scissors still play an important role in the patchwork process. You will need a pair of large fabric scissors to easily cut through fabric, some little thread-snipping scissors and a pair of all-purpose paper scissors for everything else. Don't use your fabric scissors for anything other than fabric as doing so will dull the blades.

Pins + clips

The best all-purpose pins for quilting have multicolored glass heads – this means that they are easy to find and the glass won't melt when you are using your iron. Sewing clips are easy to apply and will help hold many layers of fabric together while you are sewing on your binding. You will find that you use these for many other odd jobs around your sewing space too.

Seam ripper

Sometimes you must un-sew! Seam rippers have a sharp, fine tip to run under a stitch and a cutting surface at the end of the fork. This tool gently breaks the thread which allows you to undo a sewn line of stitching.

Erasable or disappearing fabric marker

This is used to temporarily mark fabric. There are erasable and washable types available in a variety of colors so that they are easy to see on the fabric surface. It's important to use a marker that has been specifically designed for use on fabrics. I like the purple air-erasable Sewline pen, as it's dark enough to see and doesn't disappear too quickly. Try a few to find a brand you like.

Basting pins or spray

When layering the backing fabric, batting and quilt top together, you will need to temporarily attach the layers prior to quilting. This is called basting (see page 14). Curved safety pins or basting spray can be used to secure the layers.

Wide washi or painter's tape

Washi tape can be used to indicate the distance ¼″ away from the needle on your sewing machine bed to aid in maintaining an accurate **seam allowance**. A small amount of space is lost to the thread in the seam and the turn of the cloth, so what yields an accurate block is often a scant ¼″ seam (or a seam just a small amount less than a ¼″) to allow for the space lost. You can test this by cutting two pieces of fabric the same size, sewing along opposite sides, and then measuring the center piece to ensure it is exactly ½″ smaller. Repeat the process until the area between the two sewn lines is accurate, adjusting your machine settings/tape marking as needed. Painter's tape can be used for temporarily marking quilting lines on your quilt top. It has a lighter adhesive, so won't leave behind any residue.

Glue stick

Apply a little glue to keep fabric in place during English (see page 84) and foundation (see page 92) paper piecing. Use a specialty fabric glue pen or an inexpensive washable glue stick.

Template plastic + fine-tip permanent marker

These are used to prepare templates for appliqué (see page 76) and English paper piecing (see page 84). Be sure to cut the template plastic using your all-purpose scissors, not your fabric scissors.

Paper

We will use this for foundation paper piecing (see page 92). Standard copy paper is fine. The thinner, the better.

Spray starch or starch alternative

Using starch, or an alternative, helps keep fabrics and quilt blocks flat and aids precision.

Iron + ironing board

Choose an iron that allows you to turn off the steam and an ironing board that isn't too soft to allow for firm pressing and flat seams.

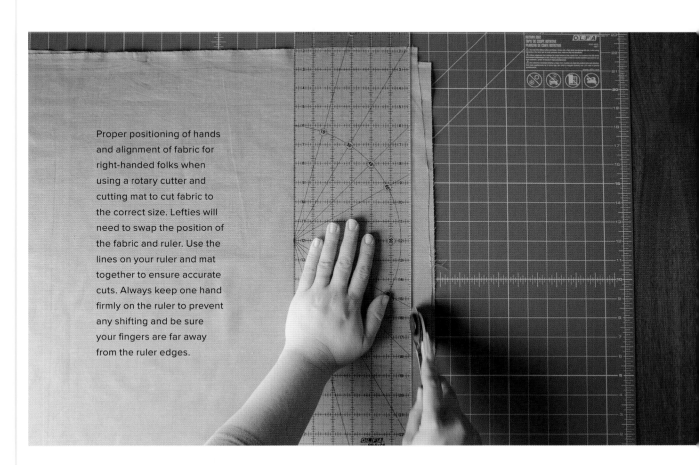

Proper positioning of hands and alignment of fabric for right-handed folks when using a rotary cutter and cutting mat to cut fabric to the correct size. Lefties will need to swap the position of the fabric and ruler. Use the lines on your ruler and mat together to ensure accurate cuts. Always keep one hand firmly on the ruler to prevent any shifting and be sure your fingers are far away from the ruler edges.

Patchwork Techniques

There are a few useful terms and techniques to know before you begin quilting. All of these and more can be explored in detail by downloading the Free Quiltmaking Basics on the Lucky Spool website.

Working With Fabric

A yard of fabric is 36˝ × WOF. The abbreviation WOF means 'width of fabric' and refers to the total width from **selvage** to selvage. Most quilting cotton fabrics are sold by the yard and are folded in half on a cardboard bolt. They measure at least 42˝ wide which is the WOF measurement my instructions use throughout.

When cutting fabric from yardage, it's important to ignore the fold from the bolt and align the selvages yourself so that the fabric hangs straight and even. Once you do this, trim away the excess fabric from one raw edge so that you are cutting from a straight edge, then cut your required pieces. Cutting mats and rulers may differ ever so slightly in the measurements, so use the mat lines to make sure the fabric is sitting straight and use the ruler markings to measure the fabric. Measure twice, cut once!

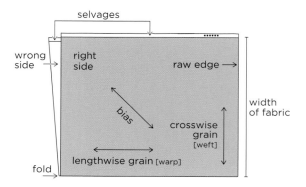

The anatomy of a yard of fabric

Fabric is made by weaving together fibers in both the lengthwise and crosswise grain (the warp and the weft). Be sure to always cut your fabric along the crosswise or straight of grain to avoid distortion. The diagonal of the warp and weft is called the 'bias' and it has a lot of give and stretch. Finally, there is also a right and wrong side of fabrics. With a printed fabric, this is easy to see but with a solid fabric of a single color, there may be no difference. All fabrics are joined by matching the right sides together before stitching.

Many patterns can use 'precuts', which are fabrics cut to a particular size by the manufacturer. These are fun because they usually contain a selection of fabrics from a single artist who designed all of them to coordinate. You can use charm squares (5˝ squares), precut 10˝ squares, fat eighths (9˝ × 21˝ cuts) and fat quarters (18˝ × 21˝ cuts) for a lot of your practice blocks and minis.

When pressing your quilt blocks, it is important to press slowly and gently, moving the iron up and down, not ironing side to side. Ironing will pull on your fabric and distort your seams. Patterns often give specific directions to press the seam allowances on the back of your piecing in a certain direction to create a more accurate finish.

What is Fussy Cutting?

Many quilts in this book include the perfect spaces for featuring fussy cut fabrics. Fussy cutting is a fantastic way to incorporate fun and personality into your quilts by carefully cutting out motifs from your fabric based on the desired finished size of your cut. There are many ways to fussy cut fabric, as shown in *The Fussy Cut Sampler* by Nichole Ramirez and Elisabeth Woo. The most common and easiest method is to center a specific motif within the cut fabric shape. It may help to use washi tape on your ruler to temporarily indicate the cut size of your shape. This creates a nice, clear window that allows you to preview the positioning before you cut. To make sure that the motif is centered, divide the width of the shape you are cutting by two. This

gives you the center line of your motif. Then, use the ruler markings to center your motif. The ¼″ seam allowance is included in this measurement, so be sure your motif won't be lost in the seam allowances.

Working With Templates and Rulers

Some quilts require making and using templates, patterns for which are located in the back of the book if you want to take a quick peek. There are many pre-made acrylic templates in some more common shapes that are available if you prefer. I often use my AccuQuilt GO! machine whenever possible to cut out the more complex shapes and curves. Many local quilt shops have these machines available to rent, so be sure to check around as these will save you a lot of time when making full-sized quilts. Otherwise, since our quilts are not too large, simply transferring the patterns onto template plastic using a fine-tipped permanent pen is really all you will need.

If the required pattern needs enlarging, photocopy the pattern by the percentage clearly marked on the pattern. Carefully trace the photocopied shape onto the template plastic using a fine-tipped pen and cut out on the drawn line. Use an erasable or disappearing fabric marker (see page 10) to trace around the template shapes onto the right side of your fabric. Cut along the drawn line using fabric scissors. All of my patterns and templates include the seam allowances (indicated in grey on the patterns), but some quilters do not include them on theirs so, be sure to read your pattern instructions carefully to double check.

Finishing Your Quilt

Batting

Batting is a layer of additional material that provides warmth, stability and texture once the three layers of your quilt (the quilt top, the batting and the quilt backing fabric—this trio is often referred to as a 'quilt sandwich') are quilted. What type of batting you choose will depend on the end purpose of the quilt. There are many fiber combinations and thicknesses (called 'loft') to choose from. If your quilt is destined to be snuggled, you'll want a softer batting like 100% cotton (lighter) or wool (warmer) as it will move and drape more easily. For the mini quilts in this book, I use Quilter's Dream 80% cotton/20% polyester as it has a slightly stiffer feel that I think is better suited to decorative mini quilts. The cut size of the batting should be 2″ larger on every side than the finished mini quilt. The excess will be trimmed away after quilting. This is because the process of adding the quilting often alters the size of the batting and backing fabrics a little.

Backing Fabric

This is the fabric that will be attached to the other side of the batting, and is often a single cut of fabric that isn't pieced. All of our minis use a yard of backing fabric to ensure complete coverage. Before basting, trim the backing so that it is about 1" larger than the batting. The trimmed quilt sandwich will be easier to move around on your sewing machine bed as you quilt.

Basting

Basting is the process of temporarily holding together the three layers of your quilt sandwich before quilting. This can be done by using safety pins or large temporary hand stitches (known as 'basting stitches') or using a basting spray or powder or curved safety pins. Before basting your project, press the finished quilt top and backing fabric to remove any wrinkles, and trim away the loose threads from the back of the quilt top.

I prefer using basting spray. If you choose to do the same, work in a well-ventilated space and carefully follow the manufacturer's instructions.

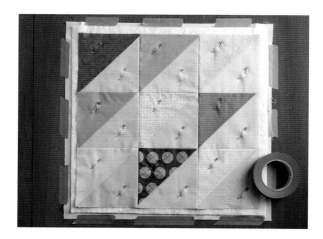

Begin by placing the backing fabric right side down on a flat, clean surface. Use wide washi or painter's tape to secure the edges down. Make sure that there are no wrinkles or puckers, but not so taut that the shape of the backing fabric is distorted. Place the batting in the center of the backing fabric and, again, smooth out any wrinkles.

If you are using basting spray or powder, fold back half of the batting and spray or sprinkle the backing fabric with the adhesive. Carefully unfold the batting from the center and work towards the edge of the fabric, smoothing out any wrinkles once more. These adhesives do not permanently stick the layers together but do keep the layers stable while you are quilting. If something isn't aligning correctly, simply lift up the offending layers and reposition as needed. Repeat this process for the other side of the batting. If you are planning to use basting stitches or safety pins to secure your layers, skip this step.

NOTE: *For many of the minis you may be able to baste all in one step instead of one half at a time.*

Place the quilt top right side up on top of the batting and repeat the same process to adhere the top to the batting. If you are not using basting spray, attach curved safety pins or use basting stitches to secure all of the layers together.

> **Q2Q** For minis, simple safety pins will be sufficient for basting, but I suggest experimenting with spray or powder basting as it is a great technique to practice in case you want to use it later for larger projects.

NOTE: *This is our first Q2Q or Quilter to Quilter note! You will find these scattered throughout the book. They are little pieces of advice from me to you...one quilter to another.*

Quilting

Quilting is the process of actually stitching your quilt sandwich together. It can be as simple or as complex as you desire, hence the common phrase, 'quilt as desired'. For beginners, this doesn't provide much inspiration. All but three of the quilts in this book were quilted on my **domestic sewing machine**. The other three were quilted by my friend, Erin from *Quilt By Starlight*, because I wanted her to use her individual style to finish them. For those I quilted myself, I included a note detailing how and why I quilted my projects as I did. Hopefully these insights will help inspire your own quilting ideas.

During the quilting process, the quilt can become a little distorted and it will need to be made as square as possible known as 'squaring up'. I use a 24½˝ ruler, and a rotary cutter over a cutting mat to carefully trim the batting and backing using the quilt top raw edges as a guide.

To square up your mini, align the ¼˝ line on the ruler with the outermost points of the quilt sandwich and trim the excess. There may be areas where the quilt top may not extend the full ¼˝, in which case, leave the batting there to make up the difference. This portion should be covered by the binding which will be attached next.

> **Q2Q** This squaring-up technique is fine for minis, but I wouldn't recommend it for larger quilts as any small differences in the width will not be noticeable at all.

Hanging Sleeve

If you plan to display your minis, whether on your own walls or as a gift, I recommend attaching a hanging sleeve to the backing before attaching the binding. This allows a rod or piece of dowel to slide through the sleeve and attach to hooks on either side. This ensures that your quilt will hang nice and straight.

For mini quilts, hanging sleeves do not need to be as big or as structured as those made for larger quilts. Prior to binding the quilt, cut a strip of fabric that is 6″ × the width of your quilt minus 2″. Hem the edges by folding the short ends in ½″, press and top-stitch in place. Fold the strip in half along the length, wrong-sides together and press. Place the strip on the back of your quilt, centered along the top edge and aligning the raw edges. Machine stitch in place using a ¼″ seam – the binding will cover that stitch line. Pin the hanging sleeve flat across your quilt back and hand-sew it down using a whipstitch (see page 85), making sure you don't stitch through to the front of your quilt. Once the sleeve is attached, add your binding as described next.

Binding

Binding is a strip of fabric usually around 2½″ wide, folded and pressed in half with the wrong sides facing. This is then attached around the perimeter of the quilt sandwich to enclose the raw edges. To attach binding on both sides using your sewing machine, sew the binding to the back side of the quilt starting in the middle of one of the sides and leaving a 3″ tail at the beginning.

When you come to a corner, stop ⅜″ away and backstitch. Rotate the quilt so that the unsewn edge is on your right. Fold the binding up away from you at a 90-degree angle.

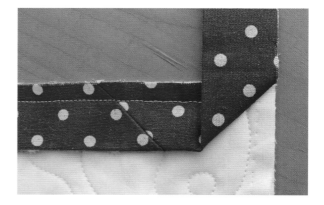

Hold the fold in place with your finger and bring the unsewn length of binding back over the fold, parallel to the unsewn edge. Continue stitching on the binding around the entire top.

When you come close to the beginning, stop a few inches away, leaving another 3″ tail of binding. Cut this end to a 45-degree angle. Unfold one end of the binding and place the cut end inside, aligning the lengthwise folds. Mark where the cut end lies on the binding below it.

Measure and cut ½˝ away from the drawn line. With the two tail ends right sides together, sew a ¼˝ seam to complete the continuous loop of binding that should fit perfectly around your quilt. Finish stitching it down on the front of the quilt. Next, attach the other folded long edge of the bias binding to the other side of the quilt. If you are attaching the binding by machine, you will be bringing the fold over to the quilt top side. If you are attaching the binding by hand, you will be bringing the fold over to the backing fabric side.

I use quilting clips to hold the binding in place, carefully folding and positioning the fabric at each corner. Choose a top thread that blends with the quilt top and a bobbin thread that matches the binding. Slowly machine stitch from the front along the ditch between the binding and the quilt top — a walking foot will make this stitching process much easier.

The alternative is to attach the binding to the backing fabric by hand using a whipstitch.

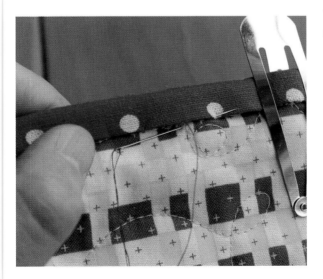

Making a Pillow Cover

Turning a mini quilt into a pillow is easy! Once it has been quilted and trimmed, cut two rectangles the width of your quilt top and two thirds the height. Fold over the long edge of each rectangle a ¼˝ then ½˝, pressing each time and enclosing the raw edge. Topstitch ⅛˝ away from the inner edge to hem the rectangles.

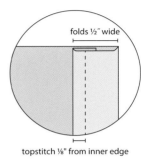

folds ½˝ wide

topstitch ⅛" from inner edge

With the right sides facing the quilt top, layer the cover rectangles over the top, aligning the raw edges; the rectangles will overlap. Sew through all the layers around the perimeter and trim the points off the corners avoiding the stitching. Turn the cover inside out and insert the appropriate size pillow form.

Alternatively, layer the cover rectangles and quilt top with the wrong sides facing and attach the binding around the raw edges.

THE
lessons

simple squares

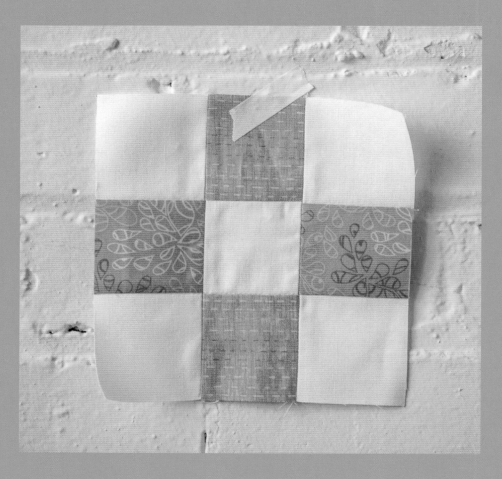

Squares. The most basic patchwork unit of all. Humble yet mighty! There is something so pleasing about the nested seams of patchworked squares or the little strips all in a row. Simple squares and rectangles can be manipulated in so many ways to make something fun and interesting. Our focus here will be on the techniques needed to make piecing them quick and efficient. We'll begin with a 9-Patch.

9-Patch Sampler Block

UNFINISHED BLOCK SIZE: 6½˝ square

FOCUS TECHNIQUE: Accurate Seams

SAMPLER NOTE: If you are making the Whirlpool Sampler on page 102, create four of these 9-Patch blocks.

Materials

Fabric A: (5) 2½˝ squares

Fabric B: (4) 2½˝ squares

> **Q2Q** Even if you do have a ¼˝ patchwork foot or marking on your sewing machine plate, it is worth checking their accuracy before you begin sewing. Even a small variation in a ¼˝ can impact the finished size over the course of piecing the entire block or mini.

Assembling the Block

1. With the right sides of a Fabric A and a Fabric B square facing each other, sew them together. Repeat to create three A/B pairs. Press the seams towards Fabric B.

2. Sew the remaining Fabric B square to the Fabric A side of one pair of squares. Press the seam towards Fabric B. To check the seam allowance accuracy, the Fabric B squares should measure 2˝.

3. Sew one Fabric A square to the Fabric B side of each of the remaining two pairs of squares. Press the seams towards Fabric B.

4. Sew the rows together to form the block. Press the seams open.

Use this block to focus on sewing accurate and straight ¼˝ seams. Once the block is sewn together and pressed, it should measure 6½˝ square. If it doesn't, try again, practicing on this quick and easy block. If your sewing machine does not have a quarter inch foot or has an inaccurate ¼˝ marking, use washi or painter's tape to indicate the ¼˝ line on your sewing machine by measuring it with your ruler.

It helps to nest the seams. When the seams are carefully pressed to opposite sides, the pressed seams butt up to each other and magically 'lock' into place. Together with an accurate ¼˝ seam allowance, this can greatly improve the accuracy of piecing so that the seams align beautifully.

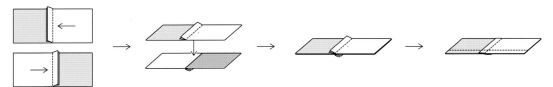

building blocks mini

FINISHED QUILT SIZE: 24″ square

UNFINISHED BLOCK SIZE: 6½″ square

I'm always looking for a way to make a quilt pattern "my own" – what can I do to personalize it? What can make it more interesting to make, what would the intended recipient like? And when that quilt is comprised of only squares, then I look to color and the fabrics to provide some extra creative challenge. Building Blocks was just crying out to be made in a rainbow and the squares were perfect for fussy cutting! I used parts of a charm pack I had on hand from a fabric swap and mixed in some other prints from my stash to get the mix of colors and designs I needed. You can be sure that the next baby that needs a quilt will be getting a fussy-cut Building Blocks quilt!

Materials

Note: Building Blocks is 5″ charm square friendly (see page 12) and is also perfect for practicing fussy cutting (see page 13). If you wish to fussy cut each square, you will need larger pieces of fabric to begin with, so that you can find the motif you want to use. How much you require depends on what part you are trying to fussy cut.

Focus Fabrics: 16 scraps measuring at least 3½″ square in a variety of colors

Secondary Fabrics: a variety of scraps measuring at least 2″ square to establish a gradient between the Focus Fabrics (see Q2Q note)

Background Fabric: ½ yard

Backing Fabric: 1 yard

Binding Fabric: ¼ yard

Batting: 28″ square

Cutting

From each of the 16 Focus Fabrics, cut:

(1) 3½″ square

From each of the 32 Secondary Fabrics, cut:

(1) 2″ square

From the Background Fabric, cut:

(32) 2″ squares

(32) 3½″ squares

From the Binding Fabric, cut:

(3) 2½″ × WOF strips

Q2Q A simple way to bring order to a scrappy quilt is by being intentional with fabric placement. Choose the 3½″ square Focus Fabrics first and use them to establish a color gradation. Next, choose Secondary Fabrics to fill in the gradient. Arrange the cut pieces following the Assembly Diagram (see page 24) and take a snapshot before assembling to use as a reference for fabric placement.

Assembling the Blocks

1. With the right sides together, align all of the raw edges and sew a 2″ Background square to each 2″ Secondary Fabric square. Press the seams towards the Secondary Fabric. Repeat to make a total of 32 pairs.

2. To create a 4-Patch unit, sew two units from Step 1 together with the right sides facing. Be sure to align the raw edges and nest the short seams. Press the long seam open. Repeat to make a total of (16) 4-Patch units.

3. With the right sides together, sew a 3½″ Background square to each 3½″ Focus Fabric square. Press the seams towards the Focus Fabric. Repeat to make a total of 16 pairs.

4. Arrange all of the assembled units on a flat surface replicating the placement in the Assembly Diagram. Pay careful attention to the orientation of the 4-Patch units. Add the 16 remaining 3½" Background squares.

5. Sew a 3½" Background square to each of the 16 assembled 4-Patch units from Step 2, keeping the orientation from Step 4. Press the seams towards the 4-Patch.

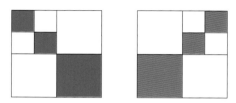

Assembling the Quilt Top

1. Referencing the Assembly Diagram, arrange the blocks into a 4x4 grid. Pay careful attention to the orientation of each block.

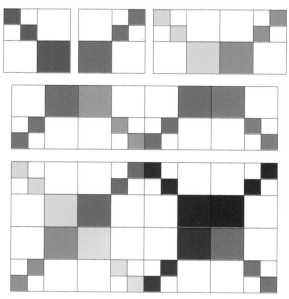

Assembly Diagram

2. Sew the blocks into four rows. Press the seams in alternate directions. This means pressing the first row of seams in one direction, the second row in the opposite direction and the next in the same direction as the first and so on. Sew the rows together. Press the seams open.

Finishing

Refer to page 14 for finishing instructions on how to baste, quilt and bind your mini quilt. Consider whether or not you want to add a hanging sleeve.

To keep the focus on the fussy cut fabrics, I chose a creamy off-white thread and quilted approximately a ¼˝ on either side of each central seam running through the blocks vertically and horizontally. Align the edge of your presser foot with the seam to keep your quilting straight.

strip piecing

When there are many identical units or blocks that contain squares or rectangles, you can often save time by piecing them together into larger strips or rows first and then subcutting to the required size. This is known as 'strip piecing' and means fewer pieces to cut and fewer seams to sew. Just as for our last practice block, keeping an accurate seam allowance here is key to avoiding an inconsistent block. I prefer to use shorter strips that are half the width of the fabric to reduce the chances of an inconsistent seam. These lengths are also more manageable for beginners.

Strips Sampler Block

UNFINISHED BLOCK SIZE: 6½″ square

FOCUS TECHNIQUE: Strip Piecing

SAMPLER NOTE: If you are making the Ripples Sampler on page 104, create four of these strip blocks.

Materials

Fabric A: (1) 8″ × 2½″ rectangle

Fabric B: (1) 8″ × 4½″ rectangle

Assembling the Block

1. With the right sides facing, sew the strips together along the 8″ width. Press the seam open. The assembled strip set should measure 8″ wide x 6½″ high.

2. Square up one end of the strip set so that the short edge is straight and square to the long edges. Subcut the strip set into three units each measuring 2½″ wide × 6½″ high.

3. Position the strips on a flat surface with all of the Fabric A cuts on the right, rotate the middle unit 180-degrees. Sew the three rows together, pressing the seams. Press the finished block well.

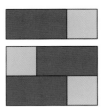

third rail

FINISHED QUILT SIZE: 21″ square

UNFINISHED BLOCK SIZE: 3½″ square

FOCUS TECHNIQUE: Strip Piecing

The Rail Fence design is a classic quilt pattern that consists of quilt blocks made from three strips of fabric. The fabrics chosen plus the way that the blocks are then arranged can create a myriad of fun quilt designs! By keeping the outer strips of each block in the same fabric, my take on the Rail Fence design creates the effect of the strip sets weaving over and under each other.

Third Rail will also put your strip piecing skills to the test! To help make it more beginner-friendly, I have recommended cutting the width of the fabric strips in half. You may also find using a walking foot (see page 8) may help as well in keeping the strips straight as will sewing more slowly.

When choosing fabrics for a quilt design like this one, it is important for there to be good contrast (or difference in colors) between the two blocks. Choosing a warm color pair and a cool one is a good way to ensure contrast, regardless of the prints (or solids) you choose.

Materials

Fabric A (dark): ¼ yard

Fabric B (light): ¼ yard

Fabric C (dark): ¼ yard

Fabric D (light): ¼ yard

Backing Fabric: 1 yard

Binding Fabric: ¼ yard

Batting: 25″ square

Cutting

From each of Fabrics A and C, cut:

- (5) 1½″ × WOF strips, subcut into:
  - (10) 1½″ × 20″ strips

From each of Fabrics B and D, cut:

- (3) 1½″ × WOF strips, subcut into:
  - (5) 1½″ × 20″ strips

From the Binding Fabric, cut:

- (3) 2½″ × WOF strips

Assembling the Blocks

1. Sew a Fabric A strip to either side of a Fabric B strip. Press the seams open. Repeat to create a total of 5 A/B/A strip sets.

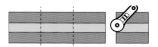

2. Trim one short end of each strip to be square. Subcut each strip set into five units measuring 3½″ square. Repeat to create a total of 25 assembled block units.

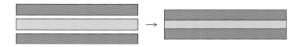

3. Repeat Steps 1-2 with the Fabric C and D strips, creating five C/D/C strip sets. Subcut a total of (24) 3½″ square assembled block units.

Q2Q When using longer strips of fabric, careful pressing is important so that the lines are completely parallel. You may find it easier to finger press first. This is when you lightly press the seam open using the pressure of your fingers before you press more flatly with your iron on a pressing board. Don't forget to experiment with some of the pressing sprays and starches available too (see page 11). These will ensure the parallel lines of your longer strip sets are nice and crisp.

Assembling the Quilt Top

1. Beginning with a Fabric A/B block in the top left corner and referencing the Assembly Diagram, alternate and rotate the blocks to create a 7 × 7 grid.

Assembly Diagram

2. Sew the blocks together into seven rows. Press the seams towards the Fabric A/B blocks. Sew the rows together nesting the seams to ensure the corners of each block match up perfectly as we practiced in Lesson 1. Press the seams open.

Finishing

Refer to page 14 for finishing instructions on how to baste, quilt and bind your mini quilt. Consider whether or not you want to add a hanging sleeve.

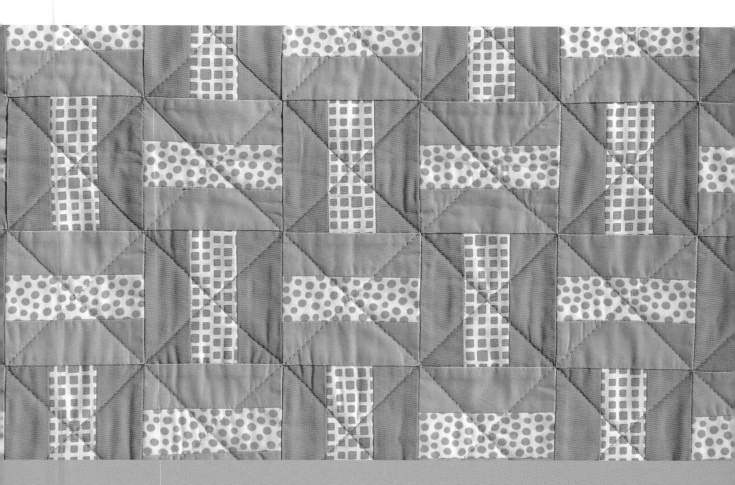

Quilting Suggestions

I kept the quilting simple by sewing along each diagonal through the quilt. I used a **hera marker** (see page 118) and a long ruler to mark the lines first so that they were straight and intersected each four-corner seam on the top. I quilted from one side to the other, always starting and stopping on the same side. Doing so eliminates maneuvering back and forth on the bed of your sewing machine. This motion often creates a slight puckering around the stitching.

snowball blocks

Square cuts of fabric don't need to remain squares as they did in Lesson 1. Simply by sewing smaller squares to each corner of a larger square (or even just one, two or three of them), a completely different block is created. When the smaller square finishes at ⅓ the size of the larger and you piece one into all four corners, this creates an octagon known as the snowball quilt block. Trimming away the excess fabric to create a seam allowance as we do in this block is a patchwork staple. The same method is used to piece Flying Geese (see page 47) or Square-in-a-Square (see page 42) blocks.

Snowball Sampler Block

UNFINISHED BLOCK SIZE: 6½″ square

FOCUS TECHNIQUE: Easy Corner Triangles

SAMPLER NOTE: If you are making the Ripples Sampler on page 104, create four of these snowball blocks.

Materials

Fabric A: (1) 3½″ square

Fabric B: (1) 3½″ square

Background Fabric: (1) 8″ square

Erasable fabric marker

Acrylic ruler with a ¼″ marking

Cutting

From the Background Fabric, cut:

(8) 1½″ squares

(2) 3½″ squares

Q2Q With such small pieces, using a light misting of a spray starch or starch alternative before you press the seams can help these little triangles lie nice and flat.

Assembling the Block

1. Using an erasable fabric marker, draw a line diagonally across the wrong side of each 1½″ Background square. Place a marked Background square right sides together in a corner of the Fabric A square, aligning the raw edges. Sew along the drawn line. Using an acrylic ruler, align the ¼″ marking along the drawn line. Use a rotary cutter to trim away the corners of both fabrics, leaving a ¼″ seam allowance. Press the seam open. Repeat on the other three corners.

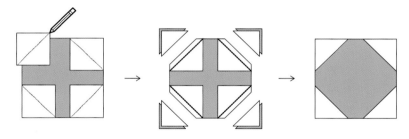

2. Repeat Step 1 for each corner of the 3½″ Fabric B square.

3. With the right sides together, sew a 3½″ Background square to each of the Fabric A and Fabric B Snowball blocks. Press the seam towards the Background square.

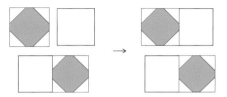

4. Sew the pairs together into a 4-Patch (see page 24), nesting the seams and press the seam open. Press the block well.

abacus

FINISHED QUILT SIZE: 21″ square

UNFINISHED BLOCK SIZE: 3½″ square

FOCUS TECHNIQUE: Easy Corner Triangles

Abacus puts together all our previous Lessons into one quilt: squares, snowball blocks and strip piecing. The name for the design was inspired by the bead-like look of the snowball blocks neatly lined up on the plus blocks – the other mathematical inspiration behind the name.

I highly recommend using some washi tape to mark a line on your machine (see page 10) instead of having to mark all the background squares for the easy corner triangles. Place the tape on the sewing machine bed so that one edge of the washi tape lines up with the needle. When sewing, line up the diagonals of your squares so that the opposing corners are on top of the edge of the washi tape. The washi tape acts as a guide for the seam, without needing to mark lines on the back of every square.

Materials

Fabric A (Snowballs): ¼ yard

Fabric B (Pluses): ¼ yard

Background Fabric: ½ yard

Backing Fabric: ¾ yard

Binding Fabric: ¼ yard

Batting: 25″ square

Erasable fabric marker or washi tape

Cutting

From Fabric A, cut:

 (2) 3½″ × WOF strips subcut into:

  (20) 3½″ squares

From Fabric B, cut:

 (4) 1½″ × WOF strips, subcut into:

  (3) 1½″ × 19″ strips

  (17) 1½″ × 3½″ rectangles

From the Background Fabric, cut:

 (7) 1½″ × WOF strips*, subcut into:

  (6) 1½″ × 19″ strips

  (80) 1½″ squares

 (1) 3½″ × WOF strip, subcut into:

  (2) 3½″ × 9½″ rectangles

  (2) 3½″ × 6½″ rectangles

  (2) 3½″ squares

From the Binding Fabric, cut:

 (3) 2½″ × WOF strips

*If your Background Fabric has more than 40″ usable inches from selvage to selvage, you may only need six strips.

COLOR PLAY

The Abacus design is graphic, with the sharp lines cutting across the background. Using a monochromatic color palette of grey emphasizes these interesting angles. If the snowball blocks and plus blocks were different colors, the quilt would look quite different, as you would see the two different blocks more clearly instead of concentrating on the lines they produce.

Assembling the Blocks

1. Using an erasable fabric pen, draw a line diagonally across the wrong side of each 1½″ Background square (skip this step if you have used the optional washi tape to mark the needle line on your machine, see page 10).

2. With the right sides together, position a 1½″ Background square in a corner of a Fabric A square, aligning the raw edges. Sew along the marked line. Following the instructions in the practice block (see page 21), trim ¼″ away from the sewn line through both of the layers. Press the seam open. Repeat for each corner of the Fabric A square.

3. Repeat Step 2 for a total of 20 Snowball blocks.

4. Sew a 19″ Background strip to both sides of a Fabric B strip and press the seams open. Repeat with the remaining strips. Following the instructions in the Strip Piecing Sampler Block (see page 27), subcut the strips into (34) 1½″ × 3½″ strip sets.

5. Sew a strip set unit to each side of the 1½″ × 3½″ Fabric B rectangles, along the long edge. Press the seams towards Fabric B. The Plus blocks should measure 3½″ square.

6. Repeat to create a total of 17 Plus blocks.

Assembling the Quilt Top

1. Referencing the Assembly Diagram, arrange the Background rectangles, the Snowball blocks and the Plus blocks to form the Abacus design.

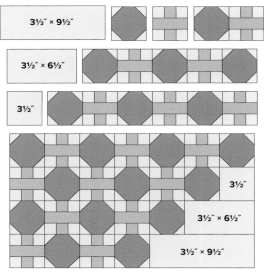

Assembly Diagram

2. Sew the units into rows. Press the seams towards the Snowball blocks. Sew the rows together. Press the seams open.

Q2Q If you would like to make a larger version of this quilt, consider repeating the instructions above to create (12) 21″ finished blocks and arrange them in a 3 × 4 grid. This will create a 63″ × 84″ quilt top.

Finishing

Refer to page 14 for finishing instructions on how to baste, quilt and bind your mini quilt. Consider whether or not you want to add a hanging sleeve.

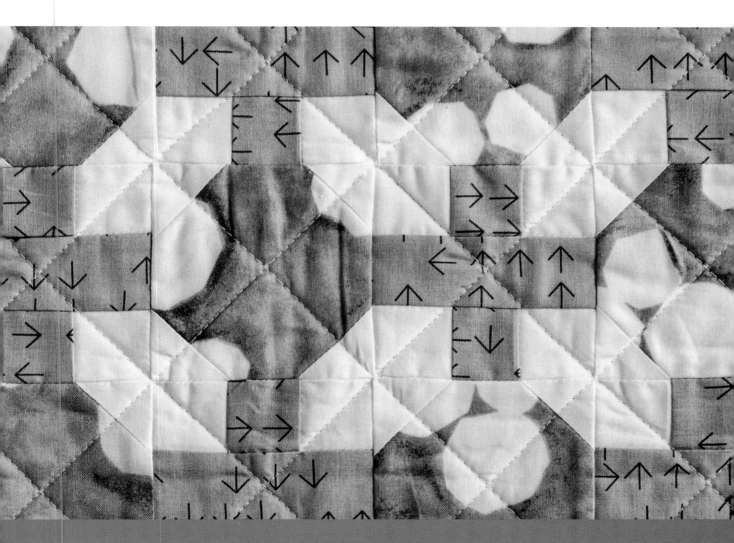

Quilting Suggestions

To emphasize the diagonal design of the quilt top, I repeated the same quilting process as for *Third Rail*. I used a hera marker and a long ruler to create creased diagonal lines using the piecing intersections of the blocks as a guide and quilted a crosshatch design.

triangles

Adding triangles creates a whole new dynamic to any project and they couldn't be simpler with the skills you have already learned. By adding angles, our eyes move around the quilt differently than if it were just squares or rectangles. One of the easiest ways to incorporate triangles into blocks is to create a square-shaped unit formed by sewing together two triangles. In patchwork, this is known as a Half-Square Triangle, or HST. Whether used on their own in large finished sizes, or as small units in a more complex quilt block, triangles provide endless design opportunities.

Half-Square Triangle (HST)

UNFINISHED BLOCK SIZE: 6½″ square

FOCUS TECHNIQUE: Half-Square Triangles, Two-at-a-Time

SAMPLER NOTE: If you are making the Whirlpool Sampler on page 102, create four of these HST 9-Patch blocks.

There are a variety of methods that can be used to piece HSTs, including different ways of making bulk amounts of them in one go. For this 9-Patch block, I'll show you how to make the HSTs using a two-at-a-time technique from two of our familiar squares of fabric. This technique is similar to the method used to make the snowball blocks in the practice block from Lesson 4 (see page 32).

Materials

Fabric A: (2) 3″ squares

Fabric B: (1) 2½″ square

Background Fabric: 10″ square

Erasable fabric marker

Acrylic ruler with a 45-degree angle marking

Cutting

From the Background Fabric, cut:
  (2) 3″ squares
  (4) 2½″ squares

> **Q2Q** I often create unfinished HSTs that are slightly larger than I will need and then trim them down to the perfect size. HSTs can be easily distorted when cutting and pressing because they are sewn on the bias (see page 12). Once trimmed, try to handle them as little as possible to reduce the chances of stretching.

Assembling the Block

1. Using an erasable fabric marker, draw a diagonal line on the wrong side of a 3″ Background square. Place a Fabric A and a marked 3″ Background square right sides together. Sew ¼″ away from both sides of the line.

2. Cut along the line and press the seams towards Fabric A. Repeat to make 4 Half-Square Triangles.

3. Aligning the 45-degree marking on the ruler with the seam line, carefully trim each HST to 2½″ square.

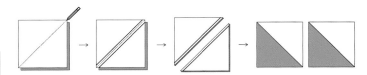

4. Arrange the HSTs, Fabric B square and the remaining 2½″ Background squares into a 9-Patch. Sew each row together and press the seams towards the Background squares.

5. Sew the three rows together, nesting the seams to ensure the corners of the squares align perfectly. Press the seams open and give the block a final pressing.

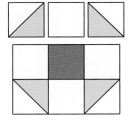

tropical sunset

FINISHED QUILT SIZE: 24″ square

FOCUS TECHNIQUE: HSTs — Eight-at-a-Time Method

My all-time favorite quilt block designs are stars, which probably stems from my long-time love of all things celestial! The sawtooth star is the center block in Tropical Sunset. It is a great, basic quilt block which I use as the starting place for many of my quilt designs. The design of the rest of the mini began with the HSTs exploding away from the centered sawtooth star. To fill the leftover space, a square-in-a-square block (also known as an economy block) was the answer to maintain the flow of the geometric explosion. The central squares are perfect for fussy cutting a favorite fabric!

Tropical Sunset uses a method of making HSTs that results in eight HSTs from two squares of fabric. This technique is efficient when there are many, identical HSTs to make. By using prints that are darker for the middle HSTs and lighter for the outer HSTs, it emphasizes the exploding effect.

Materials

Fabric A (purple): 1 fat eighth

Fabric B (pink): 1 fat eighth

Fabric C (dark mustard): 1 fat eighth

Fabric D (light mustard): 1 fat eighth

Background Fabric: ⅔ yard

Backing Fabric: 1 yard

Binding Fabric: ¼ yard

Batting: 28″ square

Erasable fabric marker

Cutting

From Fabric A, cut:

(1) 4½″ square

(1) 6″ square

From Fabric B, cut:

(4) 4½″ squares

From Fabric C, cut:

(4) 2½″ squares

(1) 6″ square

From Fabric D, cut:

(4) 2½″ squares

(2) 6″ squares

From the Background Fabric, cut:

(6) 2½″ × WOF strips subcut, from longest to narrowest, into:

(4) 2½″ × 10½″ rectangles

(4) 2½″ × 8½″ rectangles

(12) 2½″ × 4½″ rectangles

(28) 2½″ squares

(1) 6″ × WOF strip subcut into:

(4) 6″ squares

From the Binding Fabric, cut:

(3) 2½″ × WOF strips

> **Q2Q** While the HST is a simple block to make, maintaining the correct orientation of each unit when they are pieced into a larger block can take some concentration. Be sure to reference the Assembly Diagrams as you go to ensure the proper rotation of the background fabric as you assemble this mini.

Assembling the HSTs

1. On the wrong side of each 6″ Background square, draw two diagonal lines to form an 'X'.

2. Position the marked Background square from Step 1 and a 6″ Fabric C square right sides together aligning the raw edges. Sew ¼″ away from each drawn line, on both sides of the line.

3. Cut along the drawn lines and along the vertical and horizontal centers. Press the seams towards Fabric C and trim the eight resulting HSTs to 2½″ square.

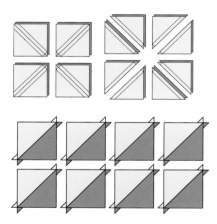

4. Repeat Steps 1-3 for the 6″ Fabric A and D squares. This will result in eight Fabric A HSTs and sixteen Fabric D HSTs.

Assembling the Square-in-a-Square Units

1. Follow the instructions for creating a Snowball unit (see page 32) using the four Fabric B squares and the 2½″ Background squares. The larger Background squares will frame the Fabric B square instead of creating an octagon. Attach Background squares to two opposite corners first (the squares will overlap in the middle).

2. Trim away the excess fabric leaving a ¼″ seam allowance. Press the triangles open.

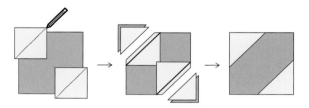

3. Attach the remaining two Background squares to the other two corners of the Fabric B square. Trim away the excess fabric leaving a ¼″ seam allowance. Press the triangles open.

4. Repeat Steps 1-3 to create a total of four Square-in-a-Square units.

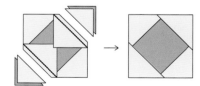

Assembling the Sections

1. Referencing the Section 1 Assembly Diagram for orientation, attach two Fabric A HSTs and press.

2. Assemble a row using the unit from Step 1, two 2½″ × 4½″ Background rectangles, and a Square-in-a-Square unit.

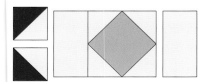

Section 1 Assembly Diagram

3. Repeat Steps 1 and 2 to create four Section 1 units.

4. Create a 4-Patch (see page 24) using two Fabric C HSTs, a 2½″ Background square and a 2½″ Fabric D square. Press the seams open.

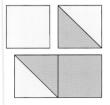

5. Sew together a Fabric D HST to the left and a Fabric C HST to the right of a 2½″ Background square. Press the seams towards the Background Fabric.

6. Sew together a Fabric D HST, a 2½″ Background square, a Fabric C HST and a Fabric C square as shown, to form a row.

7. Gather a 4½″, 6½″, 8½″ and 10½″ Background rectangle. On a flat surface and referencing the Section 2 Assembly Diagram, arrange the units from Steps 4-6 and the Background rectangles into Section 2.

8. Sew the 4½″ rectangle to the 4-Patch from Step 4, then attach the 6½″ rectangle. Press the seams towards the Background rectangles.

9. Sew the assembled unit from Step 5 to the right, then attach the unit from Step 6 to the bottom. Press the seams open.

10. Sew the 8½″ Background rectangle to the right. Press. Sew the 10½″ Background rectangle to the bottom to complete the Section 2 unit.

11. Repeat to create four Section 2 units.

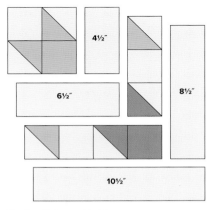

Section 2 Assembly Diagram

43

Assembling the Quilt Top

Referencing the Assembly Diagram, arrange the assembled sections around the Fabric A square. Sew the sections together in three rows. Press the seams open, then sew the rows together to form the mini. Press the seams open.

Assembly Diagram

Finishing

Refer to page 14 for finishing instructions on how to baste, quilt and bind your mini quilt. Consider whether or not you want to add a hanging sleeve.

Q2Q It can be useful to create a small 'design wall' when working with sections that have a lot of smaller pieces like this mini. A large design wall can be purchased or made by covering 4′ × 8′ foam insulating panels from a hardware store with batting, but they need not be that large. Try creating a smaller one yourself. Purchase a standard 24″ × 36″ canvas from an art supply store or online. Cover it with some batting or felt and smooth it over the front of the canvas. Be sure the batting is nice and taut, turn it over and use staples to secure it to the wooden frame on the back of the canvas. Turn it over again and place a cut piece of fabric on the batting. You will find that they temporarily 'stick' to the surface due to static electricity!

Quilting Suggestions

For the quilting on Tropical sunset, I wanted to emphasize the exploding half-square triangles and keep the quilting angular. I started with the four radiating lines, before adding in the arrow shapes to fill in the spaces between the HSTs. The jagged triangle **free-motion quilting** design fills the remaining background space and the fussy cut prints are emphasized by quilting a square-in-a-square around the central motifs.

45

flying geese

By using the easy corner triangle technique from Lesson 3 but this time with rectangles, you create a block known as 'Flying Geese'. The name of the block refers to the larger triangle being the goose and the smaller triangles are the sky. This is another quilt-making staple and will add a lot of flexibility to your sewing. Flying Geese are fun to use in a variety of sizes in one quilt top to add interest and create movement.

Flying Geese Sampler Block

UNFINISHED BLOCK SIZE: 6½″ square

FOCUS TECHNIQUE: Playing with Scale

SAMPLER NOTE: If you are making the Whirlpool Sampler on page 102, create eight of these double Flying Geese blocks.

Materials

Fabric A: 3½″ × 6½″ rectangle

Fabric B: 2″ × 3½″ rectangle

Background Fabric: 10″ square

Erasable fabric marker

Cutting

From the Background Fabric, cut:
- (4) 2″ squares
- (2) 3½″ squares
- (1) 2″ × 6½″ rectangle

> **Q2Q** I'm teaching you the one-at-a-time method for making this block. There are methods that produce four units, but this one allows you to really focus on your fabric placement.

Assembling the Flying Geese

1. Using an erasable fabric marker, draw a diagonal line on the wrong side of the 2″ Background squares.

2. With the right sides together, place a marked Background square on a Fabric B rectangle corner, aligning the raw edges.

3. Sew along the marked line. Using the method on page 33, trim ¼″ away from the sewn line. Press the seam open.

4. Repeat for the remaining corner of Fabric B.

5. Repeat Steps 1-4 with two 3½″ Background squares and the Fabric A rectangle.

6. Sew a 2″ Background square to both sides of the Fabric B Flying Geese unit from Step 4. Press the seams open. Attach the Background rectangle to the bottom long edge.

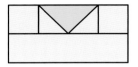

7. Sew together the assembled unit from Step 6 and the Fabric A Flying Geese. Press the seam open and give the finished block a press as well.

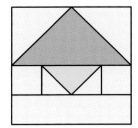

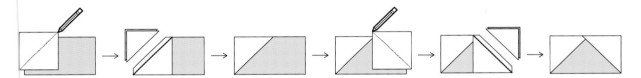

geese lightning

FINISHED QUILT SIZE: 30″ square

UNFINISHED BLOCK SIZE: 6½″ square

FOCUS TECHNIQUE: Creating Gradients

In this project, we will be exploring how value works. Value is the lightness or darkness of a fabric relative to the other fabrics you have selected. Begin by selecting five colors, one for each row in our mini. As you can see, I selected red, yellow, green, blue and purple. Next, select three prints for each row: a dark, a medium and a light value (see my tip below). Each row will be a mini gradient!

Materials

Five Dark Fabrics: ⅛ yard each

Five Medium Fabrics: ⅛ yard each

Five Light Fabrics: ⅛ yard each

Background Fabric: 1¼ yards

Backing Fabric: 1 yard

Binding Fabric: ¼ yard

Batting: 34″ square

Erasable fabric marker or washi tape (see Q2Q, below)

Q2Q To speed up piecing, adhere a strip of washi tape on your machine bed instead of having to mark all the Background squares (see page 10). Line up the edge of the tape with the machine needle. Use it as a guide to align the corners of your squares that are normally connected by a drawn line as you feed them through the machine.

Cutting

From each Dark Fabric, cut:

(5) 3½″ × 6½″ rectangles

From each Medium Fabric, cut:

(5) 2½″ × 4½″ rectangles

From each Light Fabric, cut:

(5) 1½″ × 2½″ rectangles

From the Background Fabric, cut:

(5) 3½″ × WOF strips, subcut into:

(50) 3½″ squares

(5) 2½″ × WOF strips, subcut into:

(50) 2½″ squares

(50) 1½″ x 2½″ rectangles

(5) 1½″ × WOF strips, subcut into:

(50) 1½″ squares

(50) 2½″ × 1½″ rectangles

From the Binding Fabric, cut:

(4) 2½″ × WOF strips

COLOR PLAY

Dark fabric does not have to mean a dull fabric with lots of black added. It can refer to the most saturated fabric in any collection of fabrics you have selected. A great way to try to get enough contrast between the values of your gradient is to arrange your fabric choices and take a photo using the black and white filter on a camera phone. By removing the distracting color, you are left with only their true value in relation to one another as seen in various shades of black, white and grey. The darker the grey, the more saturated your fabric is and the darker its value. The paler a fabric appears, the lighter the value it has.

Assembling the Blocks

1. Gather the (25) 3½″ × 6½″ Dark Fabric rectangles and the (50) 3½″ Background Fabric squares. Following the Flying Geese assembly instructions on page 47, create a total of 25 large Flying Geese units.

2. Repeat Step 1 for the Light and Medium colored rectangles and Background squares for a total of 25 Flying Geese units of each size.

3. Attach a 1½″ × 2½″ Background Fabric rectangle along the short edges of each Medium Flying Geese unit with the right sides together and aligning the raw edges. Sew and press the seams towards the Background.

4. Repeat Step 3 to sew a 2½″ × 1½″ Background Fabric rectangle along the short side of each Light Flying Geese unit. Press the seams towards the Background.

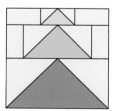

5. Arrange a large, medium and small Flying Geese unit of the same color grouping so that the Flying Geese units point in the same direction. Sew the small and medium Flying Geese units together. Press the seams towards the medium Flying Geese unit.

6. Repeat Step 5 to create 25 blocks, each containing a trio of coordinating Flying Geese.

Assembling the Quilt Top

Using a flat surface or design wall and referencing the Assembly Diagram, arrange the blocks in rows of color. Rotate the blocks 180-degrees in the alternate rows. Sew the blocks together into rows. Press the seams towards the large Flying Geese. Sew the rows together to complete the mini and press the seams open.

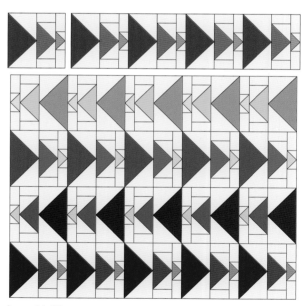

Assembly Diagram

Finishing

Refer to page 14 for finishing instructions on how to baste, quilt and bind your mini quilt. Consider whether or not you want to add a hanging sleeve.

Quilting Suggestions

I loved the zig-zag lines created by the Flying Geese across the quilt top. By stitching in the ditch around the outside of the Flying Geese and continuing the line into the Background Fabric, this exaggerates the zig-zag design. Stitching in the ditch is a machine quilting technique that involves quilting in the seam between two fabrics, aka the ditch. It hides the quilting stitches and is therefore often used to first stabilize the quilt sandwich before adding fancier quilting. In this project though, it allows continuous stitching across the quilt top.

half-rectangle triangles (HRTs)

Two right-angled triangles formed by piecing together two rectangle fabrics are known as half-rectangle triangles, or HRTs... and I'll tell you right now, this is the trickiest shape in this chapter. Unlike HSTs from Lesson 4 where the angle of the seam is always 45-degrees, the angle of the seam line in HRTs is determined by the proportions of the original rectangle. The keys to success are to make the HRTs slightly larger than required, then trim them down and use a scant ¼˝ seam (see page 54) when piecing them together.

Half-Rectangle Triangle Sampler Block

UNFINISHED BLOCK SIZE: 6½" square

FOCUS TECHNIQUE: Scant Seams

SAMPLER NOTE: If you are making the Whirlpool Sampler on page 102, create four of these double HRT blocks

Materials

Fabric A (dark): (1) 4″ × 8″ rectangle

Fabric B (light): (1) 4″ × 8″ rectangle

Background Fabric: (2) 4″ × 8″ rectangles

Assembling the Block

1. Place a Fabric A rectangle right side up on your cutting mat and cut diagonally from top right to bottom left. Repeat with one Background rectangle.

2. Place a Fabric B rectangle right side up on your cutting mat and cut diagonally from the top left to the bottom right. Repeat with the remaining Background rectangle.

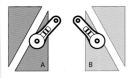

3. With a Fabric A and a Background triangle right sides together, offset the Fabric A triangle along the long diagonal edge. The smallest tip of Fabric A should extend ¼″ beyond the Background triangle at the top right and with ¼″ of the smallest tip of the Background fabric visible on the bottom left. Pin.

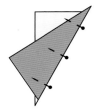

4. Carefully sew a scant ¼″ seam (see page 54) along the edge. Press the seams open.

5. Trim the HRT to 3½″ × 6½″. To trim the 3½″ width, evenly trim off the same amount from each long side of the HRT.

> **Q2Q** Positioning your ruler so that you are aligning the seams and the ¼″ ruler lines, not the edges of the ruler itself, is very important. Take your time and double-check before cutting the short side of the HRT.

6. To trim to 6½″ high, place the ruler so that the ¼″ marks from the side and top of the ruler are over the diagonal seam.

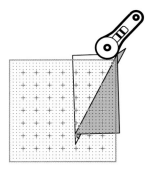

7. Trim the excess fabric from above the edge of the ruler. Repeat for the remaining short end so that the trimmed HRT measures 3½″ × 6½″.

8. Repeat Steps 3-7 with a Fabric B triangle.

9. Sew the HRT units together and press the seam open.

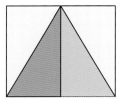

pendant

HRTs have long-been my quilty nemesis. There is no hard and fast rule guiding the mathematics of them, as they can be tall and skinny, or short and wide. The shapes that you can create with HRTs are far too beguiling to give up on them though! I particularly love the pointy diamonds that they can create when four HRTs are joined. For this mini, I had a vision of a cluster of pendant lights dangling in the air, sparkling and twinkling like stars in the sky.

Materials

Six Focus Fabrics: (1) 12″ square

Background Fabric: ½ yard

Backing Fabric: 1 yard

Binding Fabric: ¼ yard

Batting: 18″ × 34″ rectangle

COLOR PLAY

Using beautiful images found online are a great place to source color palette ideas for new projects. The fabrics for this quilt were inspired by photographs of Morocco found in Pinterest, with spicy warm colors from the buildings and markets, deep jewel tones from the textiles and the rich, bright colors of the tiles and glassware.

Cutting

From each of the six different Focus Fabrics, cut:
- (2) 3″ × 6″ rectangles

From the Background Fabric, cut:
- (12) 3″ × 6″ rectangles
- (1) 2½″ × WOF strip, subcut into:
  - (1) 2½″ x 4½″ rectangle
  - (1) 2½″ × 8½″ rectangle
  - (1) 2½″ × 14½″ rectangle
- (1) 4½″ × WOF strip, subcut into:
  - (3) 4½″ squares
  - (2) 4½″ × 6½″ rectangles
  - (1) 4½″ × 8½″ rectangle
- (1) 6½″ × 8½″ rectangle

From the Binding Fabric, cut:
- (3) 2½″ × WOF strips

Q2Q

'Scant' (see page 10 for a quick test of your machine's accuracy) means sewing the seam just slightly inside the ¼″ line and results in better accuracy for HRTs.

Piecing HRTs also involves sewing along bias edges. This means that the fabric is more likely to stretch and move out of place. Using starch and pins can help prevent movement when you practice making these units, but, instead, I recommend simply sewing slowly and handling the cut triangles as little as possible.

Assembling the Blocks

1. Unlike the Sampler Block, here we will use only one Focus Fabric for each diamond. Follow the instructions on page 53 to make (4) 2½″ × 4½″ unfinished HRTs from each of the (6) 3″ × 6″ Focus Fabric rectangles and corresponding 3″ × 6″ Background rectangles. Cut one Focus Fabric rectangle using the angle from Fabric A in our Sampler Block and the other using the angle from Fabric B. You will have two sets of HRTs that mirror each other.

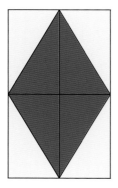

2. Referencing the Assembly Diagram for accurate orientation, position a pair of HRTs from the same Focus Fabric right sides facing. Sew together and press the seams open. Repeat for the remaining matching fabric pair of HRTs. Sew together to create a diamond and press the seams open. Repeat for the remaining five Focus Fabrics to yield a total of six pieced diamond blocks.

Assembling the Quilt Top

1. Referencing the Assembly Diagram, arrange the diamond blocks and the Background Fabrics into six sections.

2. Sew the sections together in the following order to create two horizontal panels:

Section 1 + Section 2

Section 1 & 2 + Section 3 = Panel 1

Section 4 + Section 5

Section 4 & 5 + Section 6

Section 4, 5, 6 + the 2½″ × 14½″ Background rectangle = Panel 2

3. Join Panels 1 and 2 together horizontally as shown, and press the entire top well.

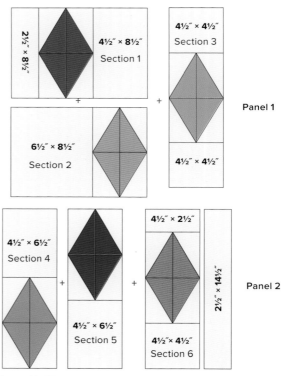

Assembly Diagram

Finishing

Refer to page 14 for finishing instructions on how to baste, quilt and bind your mini quilt. Consider whether or not you want to add a hanging sleeve.

Quilting Suggestions

This was one quilt that I knew my friend Erin would enjoy quilting on her **long arm quilting machine** and would do a beautiful job. The straight lines she stitched into the background space reinforce the idea of the diamonds dangling in the air. The point-to-point quilting within the HRT diamonds is reminiscent of the facets of beautiful glass lanterns.

simple curves

Simple curved quilt blocks use two pieces of fabric, one with a convex curve and the other with a concave curve. The classic drunkard's path quilt block is the perfect example of a simple curved quilt block and a great place to learn how to sew curves. The goal of every curved patchwork project is to create a smooth seam, free of puckers. This can be achieved using some finger pressing and a lot of pins!

Simple Drunkard's Path Sampler Block

UNFINISHED BLOCK SIZE: 6½" square

FOCUS TECHNIQUE: Creating Templates

SAMPLER NOTE: If you are making the Whirlpool Sampler on page 102, create four of these simple curves blocks

Materials

Focus Fabric: (1) 4″ × 8″ rectangle

Background Fabric: (1) 10″ square

Template plastic and a fine-tip permanent marker; or premade 3″ finished Drunkard's Path acrylic templates (see page 62)

Erasable fabric marker

Fine, sharp pins

Sharp fabric scissors

Cutting

From the Background Fabric, cut:

(2) 3½" squares

Q2Q At the pinning stage, be sure the ends of the templates, the center points, and the raw edges of the fabric are aligned. It doesn't matter how scrunched and wonky it looks, but it is important that there is no bunching of fabric within the seam allowance. Smooth the bulk of the fabric away from the edge as you sew. This time, the give in those bias edges is working for you!

1. Make templates from Drunkard's Path Patterns A and B (see page 109) and use them to trace two A shapes onto the wrong side of the Focus Fabric and two B shapes onto the wrong side of the remaining Background Fabric. Cut along the drawn lines.

2. Fold one A and one B piece in half and **finger press** to mark the center point of each shape. With the shapes right sides together and piece B facing up, align the center folds and pin the layers together.

3. Align one short end of piece B with the straight edge in the corner of piece A and pin. Repeat for the other end. Working from the center pin to each corner, slowly align the raw edges of the arcs, pinning in place as you go. It will look puckery, but it will be just fine!

4. Slowly sew a ¼″ seam around the curve, removing the pins as you go. Stop sewing with the needle down, and adjust the block to make the raw edges align when needed. Press the seam towards the Background Fabric and press the block well.

5. Repeat Steps 2-4 to make a second Drunkard's Path unit.

6. Create a 4-Patch (see page 24) using the two Drunkard's Path units and the 3½″ Background Fabric squares. Press the seams open.

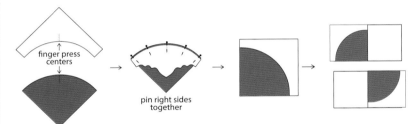

square dance

FINISHED QUILT SIZE: 24″ square

UNFINISHED BLOCK SIZE: 8½″ square

FOCUS TECHNIQUE: Piecing Pucker-Free Curves

In this mini, using two different finished sizes of the drunkard's path blocks creates a winged-bug-esque block. In my initial design, the larger Drunkard's Path units did not extend to the edge of the block, creating more space between the shapes. But once I added the contrasting lighter and darker fabrics, a secondary design appeared, and I adjusted the units to create the appearance of alternating lighter squares and darker curves.

While we are focusing on piecing pucker-free curves here, you can easily vary the size or rotation of the blocks or even add in different blocks from another lesson to create a unique mini sampler all your own. I encourage you to play around with some of your finished sample blocks and see what new and interesting designs you can create with them!

Materials

Fabric A: ¼ yard (I used dark coral)

Fabric B: ⅛ yard (I used light coral)

Fabric C: ¼ yard (I used dark blue)

Fabric D: ⅛ yard (I used light blue)

Background Fabric: ¾ yard

Backing Fabric: 1 yard

Binding Fabric: ¼ yard

Batting: 28″ square

Template plastic and a fine-tip permanent marker (4″ finished drunkard's path acrylic templates can be used for half of the blocks)

Erasable fabric marker

PREPARATION: Make A, B, C and D templates using the patterns on pages 108 and 109.

Cutting

From Fabric A, cut:
(8) Square Dance A shapes

From Fabric B, cut:
(8) Square Dance C shapes

From Fabric C, cut:
(10) Square Dance A shapes

From Fabric D, cut:
(10) Square Dance C shapes

From the Background Fabric, cut:
(18) Square Dance B shapes
(18) Square Dance D shapes

From the Binding Fabric, cut:
(3) 2½″ × WOF strips

COLOR PLAY

To create a similar secondary design of squares within your mini, choose two contrasting colors (see page 48) and a light and a dark print for each. When viewed through a black and white filter on your camera phone, the light prints and dark prints should appear to be similar shades of grey.

Assembling the Blocks

1. Pair all of the Pattern A and B shapes together. Following the instructions on page 59, create 18 small Drunkard's Path quadrant blocks. Pair all of the Pattern C and D shapes together. Create 18 large Drunkard's Path quadrant blocks.

2. Referencing the illustrations below, sew a pair of alternating large and small red Drunkard's Path quadrants into a 4-Patch (see page 24). Repeat to create a total of four Fabric A/B 4-Patches and five Fabric C/D 4-Patches.

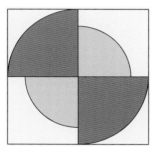

Make four A/B Square Dance Blocks

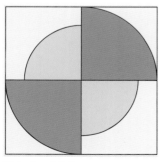

Make five C/D Square Dance Blocks

Assembling the Quilt Top

1. Referencing the Assembly Diagram and using a design wall (see page 44) or a flat surface, arrange the (9) assembled 4-Patch blocks from Step 2 into a 3 × 3 grid, alternating the order.

2. Sew the blocks into three rows and press the seams open. Sew the rows together and press the seams open again.

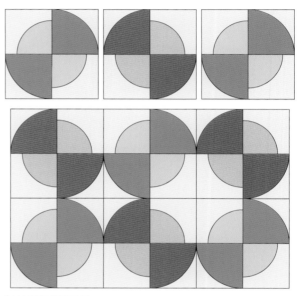

Assembly Diagram

Finishing

Refer to page 14 for finishing instructions on how to baste, quilt and bind your mini quilt. Consider whether or not you want to add a hanging sleeve.

Q2Q When making more popular blocks that require templates like this one, purchasing acrylic templates is an option. They may be a good investment if you are making many of the same sized units. To make your own, use a fine-tip permanent marker to trace the patterns onto template plastic and cut the templates out. Be sure to label each template clearly.

Quilting Suggestions

I played up the light vs. dark/square vs. circles by quilting squares in the lighter blocks and circular designs with the darker blocks. The lighter blocks were quilted approximately ¼″ inside the seams and then a smaller square in the center from curve to curve. The darker blocks were quilted approximately ¼″ from each curved edge in the background space.

complex curves

The next step after sewing a simple curved quilt block from Lesson 7 that uses two fabrics, is to use three fabrics to make one square quilt block. I refer to these designs as 'complex curves'. But that certainly doesn't mean complicated, as these are often gentler curves with lots of bias edges, which means they are easier to sew!

LET'S PRACTICE

Complex Curve Sampler Block

UNFINISHED BLOCK SIZE: 6½" square

FOCUS TECHNIQUE: Piecing Multiple Curves in One Block

SAMPLER NOTE: If you are making the Ripples Sampler on page 104, create eight of these complex curves blocks.

Materials

Focus Fabric: (1) 6½" square

Background Fabric: (1) 5" × 10" rectangle

Template plastic and a fine-tip permanent marker

Erasable fabric marker

Fine, sharp pins

Sharp fabric scissors

PREPARATION: Make A and B, Complex Curve templates using the patterns on pages 110-111.

Cutting

Using the Complex Curve templates, trace two A shapes onto the wrong side of the Background Fabric and one B shape onto the wrong side of the Focus Fabric. Using a pair of sharp fabric scissors, cut on the drawn lines.

Q2Q Try to ignore the bowtie shape of Focus Fabric and repeat exactly what we practiced on the Simple Curve block (see page 58) to complete these curves.

Assembling the Block

1. Fold each shape in half with the right sides together and finger press to create a crease at the center points.

2. With an A and B shape right sides together and with the bow tie shape (B) on top, align the center creases and pin through both of the layers.

3. Match the ends and work from the center pinning out to each edge, smoothing the fabric so the raw edges align and pinning in place as you go.

4. Slowly sew an even ¼" seam around the curve, removing the pins as you progress. Stop sewing if it seems necessary to adjust the block and make the raw edges align perfectly. If your machine has the option of a needle down position, use it to keep everything aligned as you adjust the fabrics. Press the seam towards the Background Fabric.

5. Repeat Steps 2-4 to attach the second A shape to the assembled unit from Step 4, this time keeping the A shape on top.

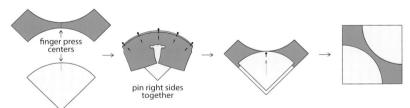

finger press centers

pin right sides together

blossom

FINISHED QUILT SIZE: 24″ square

UNFINISHED BLOCK SIZE: 12½″ square

FOCUS TECHNIQUE: Working with Multiple Curved Shapes.

The Flowering Snowball quilt block is one that I have long wanted to play with. The opportunities for playing with fabric and color placement are endless. Choosing the fabrics and colors for Blossom was, in fact, quite difficult and I ended up going with my perennial favorites, coral and mustard — two colors that always make me happy!

Materials

Fabric A: ¼ yard
(I used medium pink)

Fabric B: ¼ yard (I used dark pink)

Fabric C: ½ yard (I used mustard)

Fabric D: ½ yard (I used white)

Fabric E (center squares):
(1) 5″ square

Backing Fabric: 1 yard

Binding Fabric: ¼ yard

Batting: 28″ square

Erasable fabric marker

Template plastic and a fine-tip permanent marker

PREPARATION: Make A and B, Blossom templates using the patterns on page 112-113.

Cutting

From Fabric A, cut:
 (8) Blossom A pieces

From Fabric B, cut:
 (8) Blossom B pieces

From Fabric C, cut:
 (8) Blossom A pieces

From Fabric D, cut:
 (8) Blossom B pieces

From Fabric E, cut:
 (4) 1½″ squares

From the Binding Fabric, cut:
 (3) 2½″ × WOF strips

COLOR PLAY

One fun way to play with the fabric choices for Blossom is by choosing a color for Fabric E that sits in the middle of Fabric C and Fabric D on a typical artists' color wheel. This will create an illusion of overlapping transparent colors!

Q2Q

A walking foot, also known as a quilting foot or even-feed foot, is a sewing machine foot accessory that has in-built feed dogs. When you are using a normal sewing machine foot, the fabric is only fed through the machine's feed dogs underneath the fabric. By using a walking foot while quilting, the fabric is being evenly fed through the machine from the top and underside, reducing puckering. This is especially useful when sewing thicker or multiple layers, like a quilt sandwich. A walking foot can be purchased specifically for your make and model of sewing machine, but some come with integrated dual feed technology built into the machine. So, be sure to check your manual for your options.

Assembling the Blocks

1. Referencing the instructions on page 59, piece together a Fabric B/A/B unit by first sewing the Blossom B shape to the Blossom A shape aligning their curved edges, then attaching the remaining Blossom B shape to the opposite curved edge of the Blossom A shape. Press the seams towards the Blossom A shape.

2. Repeat Step 1 to form a total of four pieced Fabric B/A/B units and four pieced Fabric D/A/D units.

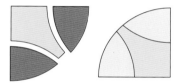

3. Pair two Fabric C Blossom B shapes with a 1½″ Fabric E square. Sew them together along their short edge and press the seams towards Fabric C. Repeat to form a total of four pieced Fabric C/E/C units.

4. Following the instructions on page 65, attach one assembled B/A/B unit and one assembled D/A/D unit to each curved edge of an assembled C/E/C unit from Step 3. Repeat to make a total of four blocks.

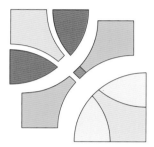

Assembling the Quilt Top

1. Referencing the Assembly Diagram, arrange the blocks into a 2 × 2 grid paying attention to the rotation of each block.

2. Sew the blocks into a 4-Patch (see page 24). Press the seams open.

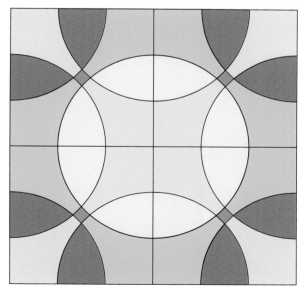

Assembly Diagram

Finishing

Refer to page 14 for finishing instructions on how to baste, quilt and bind your mini quilt. Consider whether or not you want to add a hanging sleeve.

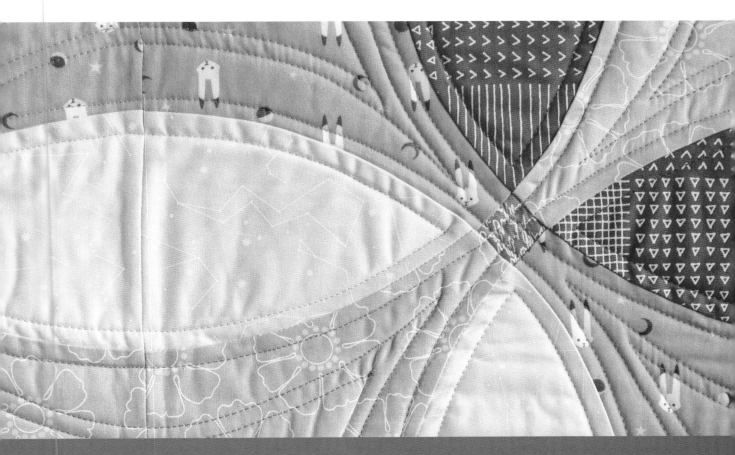

Quilting Suggestions

I wanted to keep the quilting simple to allow the shapes of the Blossom blocks to guide the eye around the quilt. To do this, I knew that I needed to reinforce the flowing curves, by first quilting approximately ¼″ away from the seam lines. I used the edge of my walking foot (see Q2Q note on page 66) as a guide. This helped to stabilize the quilt and echo the block's shape at the same time. After I finished that, I could then see that my mini needed a bit more quilting, especially in the center — partly for aesthetic reasons, partly for practical purposes to keep the quilt together and flat. Some more curved walking foot quilting in the concave pieces did the job.

improv curves

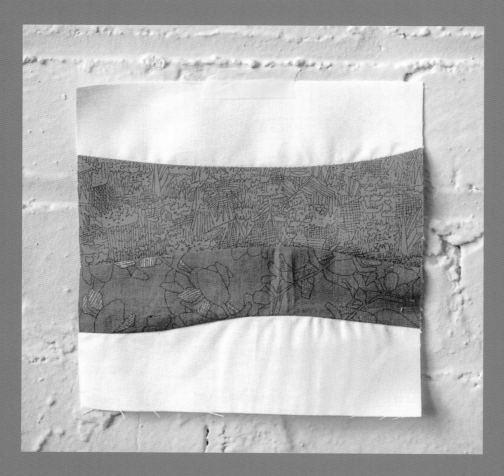

At this stage, curves should be a breeze! If you completed the Blossom Mini, I know that you can piece together any curve in any shape with ease. So let's introduce a little improvisation into our practice. There are the precise curves that require templates, accurate cutting and sewing and then there are the improv curves where your rotary cutter takes you on a unique journey every time. Improv curves are cut freehand, which means that each block will look different — some will be curvier, while others will be gentle waves. Tip — use a fresh rotary blade so that it is nice and sharp, ready to smoothly cut the fabric.

Improv Curve Sampler Block

UNFINISHED BLOCK SIZE: 6½″ square

FOCUS TECHNIQUE: Improvisational Rotary Cutting

SAMPLER NOTE: If you are making the Ripples Sampler on page 104, create four of these improv curve blocks

Materials

Fabric A: (1) 4″ × 8″ rectangle

Fabric B: (1) 4″ × 8″ rectangle

Background Fabric: 1 fat eighth

Cutting

From the Background Fabric, cut:
(2) 4″ × 8″ rectangles

Q2Q Use the needle down position if your machine has one, stopping every once in a while to carefully maneuver the fabric strip edges together as you sew. Because the curves are along the bias of the fabric, they can be gently straightened out so that you're sewing a straight seam instead of wriggling the layers back and forth. If your seam isn't sitting flat after pressing, carefully clip little V-shaped snips in the seam allowance that go in no more than halfway to the seam line.

Assembling the Block

1. On a cutting mat, position a Background rectangle over the Fabric A rectangle with both right sides facing up. Overlap the long edges by approximately 1½″. Use a rotary cutter to gently make a curvy line through both layers. Be sure to keep the cut line well within the overlapped edges.

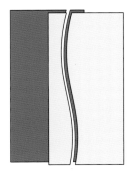

2. Discard the smaller cut strips. Place the Background and Fabric A strips right sides together and align the top corners of the cut curve.

3. Slowly sew the two strips together using a ¼″ seam allowance. With your needle down, stop sewing and reposition the fabrics as needed to be sure the raw edges align. Gently press the seam towards Fabric A.

4. Repeat Steps 1-3 using Fabric B and the remaining Background rectangle.

5. Repeat the process with the assembled units this time, and press the seams towards the darker fabric.

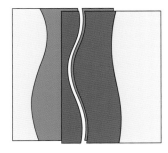

6. Press and trim to 6½″ square.

brushstrokes

FINISHED SIZE: Approximately 14″ × 25″

FOCUS TECHNIQUE: Improv Curves

As the name of this mini may suggest, the way the lines of this quilt curved across the top reminded me of wavy brush strokes across paper. With the idea of waves already simmering in my mind, I drew upon the inspiration of a beach-scape when it came to choosing the fabrics for my quilt. I chose sandy yellows and watery teals and layered them to achieve an ombré effect. I have always loved how the ocean gets darker towards the horizon and it was fun selecting just the right fabrics to create this one. What's beautiful about making one long strip of improv curved strips is that it can be as wide or as long you decide. My quilt ended up 14″ × 25″ by cutting off a 3-4″ strip from the end of a fat quarter and squaring the quilt top up to fit along a sideboard in my house. With improv curves, there are no strict guidelines!

Materials

Focus Fabrics: 11 fat quarters

Backing Fabric: 1 yard

Binding Fabric: ¼ yard

Batting: 18″ × 29″

Cutting

From each Focus Fabric, cut:

(1) 3″ strip, at least 16″ long

From the Binding Fabric, cut:

(3) 2½″ × WOF strips

COLOR PLAY

Using a large range of prints with no background fabric can get busy for your eyes to look at. Adding in a colorful solid or two provides a place for the eyes to rest, while keeping within the color palette.

Assembling the Quilt Top

1. Arrange the strips in the color order desired.

2. Take the uppermost two strips and follow the instructions for layering, cutting and piecing from our practice block for Lesson 9. Press the seam towards the darker fabric.

3. Place the third strip right side up on the cutting mat layered over the assembled unit from Step 2. Again, overlap the second and third strips by approximately 1½˝ and cut a curvy line. Sew the strips together and press the seam towards the darker fabric.

4. Repeat for the remainder of the strips following the Assembly Diagram if you are also creating a gradient.

5. Once all of the strips are attached, press the completed quilt top well, remembering to clip into the seam allowance a bit if the curves aren't lying flat. Trim one long side at a right angle to the edge of the first strip. Repeat for the remaining long side.

Finishing

Refer to page 14 for finishing instructions on how to baste, quilt and bind your mini quilt. Consider whether or not you want to add a hanging sleeve.

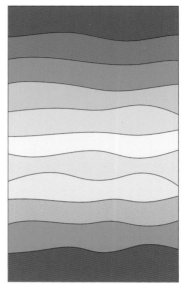

Assembly Diagram

Quilting Suggestions

Brushstrokes is another quilt that shows off the quilting. I sent mine to my long-arming friend, Erin, to let her play in the space. She divided the quilt into five sections and using a coordinating thread, quilted a different design in each section.

appliqué

Appliqué is the process of cutting fabric into shapes and then attaching the cut pieces to the top of another piece of fabric. The two fabrics can be secured together by hand or machine. With both techniques, there are a variety of methods that can be used. We'll use a machine-stitching method to create appliqué shapes where the smooth tucked-under edge of needle turn appliqué is achieved through machine stitching. This is a beginner-friendly method and will introduce a new material to play with — interfacing.

UNFINISHED BLOCK SIZE: 6½″ square

FOCUS TECHNIQUE: Using Single-Sided Fusible Interfacing.

SAMPLER NOTE: If you are making the Ripple Sampler on page 104, create one of these teardrop blocks.

Let's talk a little about the different types of interfacing. Interfacing is a material that provides strength and support to fabric, particularly in garments and bags. In quilting, we use it for appliqué to provide the firm, crisp outlines of the shapes, and to adhere the shapes to the background fabric. There are a wide range of interfacing options available, from fusible to sew-in, from non-woven to knit, and from lightweight to heavy. For quilting, and specifically appliqué, you will need a fusible interfacing. This comes with either a single- or double-sided adhesive layer that is activated by a hot iron. It depends on which method of appliqué you are using as to whether you will want the single- or double-sided variety. For our appliqué block, it only needs to have adhesive on one side.

The interfacing does not need to provide any strong stability, as it does in cuffs or bags. For this project, use a lightweight, non-woven interfacing like Pellon PLF36 or Therm O Web 3336. This means that the interfacing adds less bulk and won't stretch in one direction as woven interfacing does, so you can use any piece that best fits all of the shapes you may be creating.

Materials

Focus Fabric: 1 fat eighth

Background Fabric: 6½″ square

Fusible Interfacing (single-sided, lightweight, non-woven): 5″ × 10″

Photocopy of the Teardrop pattern (see page 114), cut out

Iron

Cutting

From the Focus Fabric, cut:

(4) 2½″ × 5″ rectangles

From the Fusible Interfacing, cut:

(4) 2½″ × 5″ rectangles

Q2Q Interfacing is often used when making bags or clothes to add stiffness to a fabric by attaching it to the wrong side of the fabric. There are many different types of interfacing available and they tend to look very similar, so be sure to ask for help in finding the one I have suggested above or include all of the description in an online search. Be sure to read the instructions on the wrapper that comes with your interfacing as it will have tips on iron settings and the suitability of fabric types for this specific interfacing.

Assembling the Block

1. Trace around the teardrop onto the wrong side of a Focus Fabric rectangle. Mark another line around the teardrop approximately ¼″ away from the first drawn line. We will be trimming down this seam allowance more accurately later, so don't worry about making a perfect ¼″ line. Cut out around the outer line. Layer the teardrop over a rectangle of Interfacing with the fusible side facing the right side of the fabric.

2. Using a slightly shorter stitch length setting than usual, sew along the inside marked line from Step 1. Trim away the excess fabric and interfacing from outside the sewn line, leaving an ⅛″ seam allowance around the appliqué. Clip into the seam allowance slightly, all the way around the teardrop through both layers.

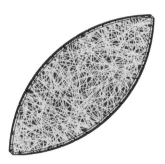

3. Using a pair of sharp scissors, carefully cut an opening approximately 2″ in length and through just the middle of the Interfacing only. Be careful not to cut the fabric layer itself.

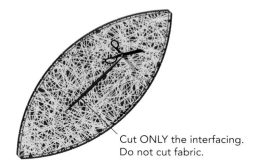

Cut ONLY the interfacing.
Do not cut fabric.

Q2Q If you are having trouble lifting away the interfacing enough to cut an opening, try using the tip of a safety pin or a regular pin to help separate the two layers.

4. Turn the fabric right side out through the opening in the Interfacing and use a pointy, blunt object like a chopstick to gently and evenly push out the corners and edges of the shape. Finger press the edges flat – do not use an iron, as it will activate the fusible in the Interfacing.

5. Repeat Steps 1-4 to create a total of four teardrop appliqués and set them aside.

6. Fold the Background square in half along both diagonals and press to create creases that cross in the center of the square.

7. Using the creases from Step 6 as a guide, arrange the appliqué shapes so that the points of the teardrop are aligned on a crease. One point should align with the center point of the square and the other will be ¼″ away from the outer corners. Pin in place.

8. Once you are happy with the position of each shape, remove the pin and carefully fuse one shape at a time to the Background fabric using a hot iron.

9. Using a thread that matches the Focus Fabric, carefully edgestitch (see the Q2Q below) around the folded edge of the shapes. Keep all of the stitching on the Focus Fabric to secure the appliqués in place, stopping, lifting up the presser foot with the needle down and pivoting the layers when you approach each teardrop tip, then continuing to sew. Press the block.

Q2Q Edgestitching is sewing very closely to the folded edge of a fabric. It is important to try to maintain the same distance away from the folded edge with your stitching. When using edgestitching for appliqué, the goal is to try to hide the stitching as near to the fold as possible, while still staying on the focus fabric. It may take a little practice to get the hang of it. Stitch slowly and use an open-toe acrylic sewing machine foot if you have one, so that you can see exactly where you are stitching. See page 80 to choose an appropriate stitch style for edgestitching.

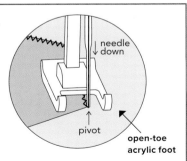

rising sun

FINISHED QUILT SIZE: 20″ square

UNFINISHED BLOCK SIZE: 4½″ square

FOCUS TECHNIQUE: Raw-Edge Machine Appliqué

My family lived in Japan for four years. While the fabric shopping is definitely amazing, now that we are back home in Australia, we miss those little moments in our daily life, local shops and favorite restaurants that were only to be found in the suburbs of Chiba, Japan. This mini serves as a reminder of our favorites: bakeries, enjoying the seasonal decorations in stores, that first glimpse of Mount Fuji across Tokyo Bay after the humid summer haze had faded... Japan was where I truly fell in love with quilting too, so it was a no-brainer to use red fabrics for the circles in Rising Sun.

I find raw edge appliqué to be more precise when sewing circles, as there are no tucked-under edges to smooth out perfectly to maintain the shape. Some stitch options your machine may have that are suitable for machine appliqué are shown below. The stitch is usually determined by the shape. For curved shapes, I prefer to use a straight edgestitch (see the Q2Q on page 79) and carefully sew around the appliqué three times to secure it. This layered stitching also introduces a bit of texture. What matters most in machine appliqué projects, is that you use a matching thread color or a monofilament thread and keep the stitches just on the edge so that they are nearly invisible.

Materials

Fabric A: ⅓ yard (I used light grey)

Fabric B: ⅓ yard (I used dark grey)

Fabric C (circles): ¼ yard

Fabric D (circles): ¼ yard

Backing Fabric: 1 yard

Binding Fabric: ¼ yard

Batting: 24″ square

Double-sided, lightweight, fusible Interfacing (17″ wide): ¾ yard

Erasable fabric marker & pencil

Fabric scissors

Iron

Cutting

From each of Fabrics A and B, cut:

(2) 5″ × WOF strips, subcut into:

    (13) 5″ squares

From Fabric C, cut:

(2) 3½″ × 25″ strips

From Fabric D, cut:

(2) 3½″ × 22″ strips

From the Interfacing, cut:

(2) 3½″ × 25″ strips

(2) 3½″ × 22″ strips

From the Binding Fabric, cut:

(3) 2½″ × WOF strips

Straight stitch, edgestitching

Blind Hem stitch

Zig-zag stitches

Variety of possible appliqué stitches you may have on your machine

Assembling the Blocks

1. Using the Fabric A and B squares, make 25 HSTs (see page 39) and trim them down to 4½" squares.

2. Following the manufacturer's instructions, apply the Interfacing strips to the wrong sides of Fabrics C and D. Subcut Fabric C into (13) 3½" squares and Fabric D into (12) 3½" squares.

3. Using the Rising Sun pattern (see page 117) and a pencil, trace a 3" circle onto the paper side of the interfaced Fabric C and D squares and cut them out with fabric scissors. Peel the paper away from one circle. With both right sides up, place the circle in the center of an HST from Step 2, approximately ¾" from each edge. Fuse in place. Repeat for each Fabric C and D interfaced circle.

4. Use a thread that matches the Circle fabric and edgestitch three times around each edge of the circle as close to the edge as possible.

Assembling the Quilt Top

1. Arrange the appliquéd HSTs into a 5 × 5 grid following the Assembly Diagram, alternating the Fabric C and D prints.

2. Sew the HSTs into rows. Press the seams in alternate directions. Sew the rows together, nesting the seams and press them open.

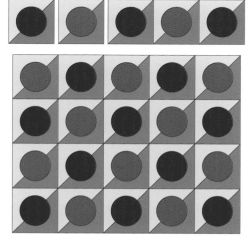

Assembly Diagram

Finishing

Refer to page 14 for finishing instructions on how to baste, quilt and bind your mini quilt. Consider whether or not you want to add a hanging sleeve.

Quilting Suggestions

To make the circles really pop, quilt around the outside edge of the circles. This gives the illusion that they have puffed up a little. I quilted one half of the quilt approximately ¼″ from the left side of each diagonal seam and around the circle in a thread that matched the lighter background. Then I repeated the same for the right side of each diagonal seam and around the circle in the other half, using a darker thread.

english paper piecing

English paper piecing, or EPP, is a method whereby fabric is basted onto a lightweight cardstock or other thick paper. The shapes are then whipstitched together by hand to create a quilt block. You can create many English paper pieced blocks and then sew them together, just like a standard quilt, or you can make individual blocks and appliqué those onto the background fabric as you work. This is the perfect portable project!

English Paper Piecing Sampler Block

UNFINISHED BLOCK SIZE: 6½˝ square

FOCUS TECHNIQUE: English Paper Piecing

SAMPLER NOTE: If you are making the Whirlpool Sampler on page 102, create one of these EPP star blocks

The paper pieces for EPP, like the pattern for this block on page 114, won't have a seam allowance included. This means that when you are cutting out the fabric for your shape, you will need to add some extra around the shape for your seam allowance. If you are a beginner, you will find a ⅜˝ seam allowance more forgiving when it comes to basting, otherwise add the standard ¼˝ seam allowance around the fabric shape before cutting. This doesn't have to be exact and the edges will be turned under, so you can just eyeball the required seam allowance or measure and mark ¼˝ around each shape using an erasable pen.

Materials

Fabrics A and B: (2) 4˝ squares

Background Fabric: (1) 6½˝ square

Size 9 milliners or straw needle

50-weight thread

Glue pen

Quilting clips

Four copies of the EPP Kite (see page 114) on cardstock

Iron

Erasable marking pen (optional)

Cuticle stick (optional)

Cutting

Using Fabrics A and B, cut from each:
  2 EPP Sampler Kite + seam allowance pieces

Q2Q Whipstitching is a simple stitch commonly used to sew EPP projects. To attach the shapes, place two basted shapes (see page 86) right-sides together and use a quilting clip to hold them firmly in place. Insert the needle from one side through both fabrics in the folds in the corner of your shapes. Pull the needle through to the other side and insert it back into the starting hole again. Pull the needle through to the other side, and as the thread creates a loop and begins to tighten, thread the needle through that loop and pull to make a knot. Stitch your way down the length of the side – insert the needle perpendicular to the fabric from one side, and pull through to the other side. Because I am right handed, I hold the shapes in my left hand, and insert the needle from right to left, but experiment and see what's more comfortable for you.

Q2Q Glue basting EPP shapes is like gift wrapping a present – you want crisp folds and edges. Position the cardstock in the middle of the wrong side of a Fabric A shape. Working on one edge at a time, add a thin strip of glue along one edge of the paper. Fold over that edge of the fabric onto the paper butting it up against the paper's edge. Use the edge of the paper to get a nice, crisp, straight fold. When you get to a corner, baste the first edge as before, and then add another little dab of glue to the top of the first fabric fold, as well as to the next edge of the fold. This will keep the next edge of fabric firmly basted too. When you have folded over all of the edges around your shape, turn the fabric right side up and make sure it is free of any puckers and looks nice and smooth.

Assembling the Block

1. Place a cut Fabric A kite shape right side down on a flat surface. Place the paper kite on top, centered within the fabric, with the paper facing the wrong side of the fabric. Run a small swipe of glue along one edge of the paper and carefully fold the edge of the fabric over the paper. Use your fingers to press it down onto the glue. The fabric should be taut, but not bending the shape. Repeat for each edge of the paper kite.

2. Repeat Step 1 to make the two EPP kites from each of Fabrics A and B for a total of four kites.

3. Position a Fabric A and B kite, right sides facing. Use a quilting clip to hold them firmly together. Whipstitch (see the Q2Q on page 85) from point-to-point along the shortest side, making a knot at the start and end of each seam. Repeat to make a second Fabric A/B pair.

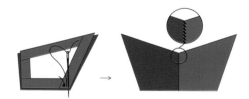

4. Whipstitch the pairs together to create a star shape.

5. Place the star right side down on a pressing surface. Press firmly to crease the seam allowances in place. Gently remove the papers from the back of the star. A cuticle stick or similar may help to flick the papers out. Carefully press the seam allowances flat again without distorting the shape of the star.

6. Fold the Background square in half diagonally twice and press to create creases at the half-way points in the square.

7. Using the creases from Step 6 as a guide, arrange the shape so that the points of the star are aligned on the creases.

8. Use a matching thread and edgestitch the star in place. If there is an excess of fabric known as dog ears (see the Q2Q below) sticking out at the points of the stars, trim them a little shorter and tuck them underneath the star before sewing the EPP unit to the Background square. Press the block well.

Lesson 11: English Paper Piecing

carpenter's diamond

FINISHED QUILT SIZE: 18″ square

FOCUS TECHNIQUE: Piecing a Complex Pattern.

My love affair with star quilt blocks continues into English paper piecing too. Carpenter's Diamond is based on the traditional carpenter's star quilt block, but by using EPP to construct it, it allows for more complex shapes without fiddly machine piecing.

EPP is a great opportunity to fussy cut small motifs or directional fabrics which can create visual interest and movement across the quilt top. Use this mini quilt as an opportunity to show off your fussy cutting and color choosing skills! Pay careful attention to which direction the shapes are pointing in the quilt top if you are fussy cutting directional fabrics — half of the purple spot diamonds in my quilt had to be cut one way, and the other half as the mirror image.

Materials

Orange Fabric A: 1 fat eighth

Light Pink Fabric B: 1 fat eighth

Coral Fabric C: 1 fat eighth

Bright Pink Fabric D: 1 fat eighth

Dark Purple Fabric E: 1 fat eighth

Purple Fabric F: 1 fat eighth

Teal Fabric G: 1 fat eighth

White Background Fabric:
1 fat eighth

32 copies of the Carpenter's Diamond Pattern A (see page 114)

32 copies of the Carpenter's Diamond Pattern B (see page 114)

4 copies of the Carpenter's Diamond Pattern C (see page 114)

Backing Fabric: 1 yard

Binding Fabric: ¼ yard

Batting: 22″ square

Size 9 milliners or straw needle

50-weight thread

Glue pen

Quilting clips

Cardstock

Cutting

Remember to include ¼″ to ⅜″ seam allowance around each paper when cutting.

From the Orange and Light Pink Fabrics, cut:
  4 Pattern A shapes

From the Coral Fabric, cut:
  8 Pattern B shapes

From the Bright Pink, Dark Purple and Purple Fabrics, cut:
  8 Pattern A shapes

From the Teal Fabric, cut:
  4 Pattern C shapes

From the Background Fabric, cut:
  24 Pattern B shapes

From the Binding Fabric, cut:
  (3) 2½″ × WOF strips

Q2Q Take your fussy cutting to the next level! Create clear plastic templates of the patterns by tracing around the copied patterns A-G and adding a seam allowance. Use the templates as a window to easily find the motifs you would like to fussy cut.

Assembling the Block

1. Following the instructions on page 86, glue-baste all the fabric cuts to their respective papers.

2. Pair an Orange and Light Pink template A diamond, right sides together and clip into place. Whipstitch along one side. Sew a template B Background triangle to each pair by first sewing along one short edge of the triangle, then folding the assembled pieces to attach the second side.

3. Repeat Step 2 to create a total of four units and attach the four assembled units together to form the center star.

4. Pair four Coral template B triangles with template B Background triangles, forming a Half-Square Triangle. Attach to the unit from Step 3 and set the center star aside.

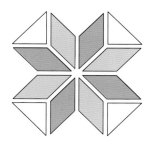

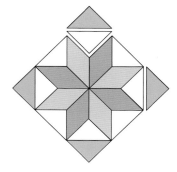

5. Repeat Step 2 with the Bright Pink and Light Purple template A diamonds and template B Background triangles and also with the Dark Purple diamonds and template B Coral triangles. Separate the units into four sets of trios.

6. Attach one trio set from Step 5 according to the diagram. Attach two, template B Background triangles to the diamond trio. Finally attach a large Teal template C triangle. Repeat to make a total of four corner units.

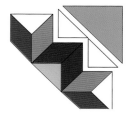

7. Referencing the Assembly Diagram, arrange the five assembled units on a flat surface. Sew the corner units from Step 6 to the assembled center star unit from Step 4.

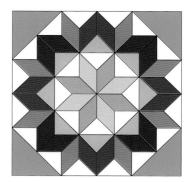

Assembly Diagram

8. Press the back of the block firmly. Gently remove the papers and press again to ensure all the inner seam allowances are crisp.

9. Unfold the seam allowances around the outside edges of the mini and press the top well.

Finishing

Refer to page 14 for finishing instructions on how to baste, quilt and bind your mini quilt. Consider whether or not you want to add a hanging sleeve.

Quilting Suggestions

Quilting point-to-point, or dot-to-dot, is where you quilt straight lines across the quilt, pivoting at various places by using marked reference points on the quilt. I used this method to create diamonds and triangles throughout the shapes, as well as some outlining and echoing.

foundation paper piecing

Our last Lesson! We have practiced creating accurate piecing from fabrics cut to precise sizes. For our last block I am showing you another way to ensure accurate piecing using imprecisely cut fabrics. It's called foundation paper piecing. It's like sewing by number! Here, larger fabric cuts are sewn onto a paper foundation and then excess fabric is trimmed away. What can take a little bit of getting used to is that the front of the paper is actually the back of the block—so you are piecing a mirror image of the printed paper. Before we begin, shorten the stitch length on your machine to 1.0 – 1.5 and remember to backstitch at the start and end of each seam.

Foundation Paper Piecing Sampler Block

UNFINISHED BLOCK SIZE: 6½" square

FOCUS TECHNIQUE: Sewing Through Paper and Working in Reverse

SAMPLER NOTE: If you are making the Ripples Sampler on page 104, create four of these foundation paper blocks.

Materials

Fabric A: approximately a 3" × 10" rectangle for Section 1

Fabric B: approximately a 4" × 10" rectangle

Background Fabric: 1 fat eighth

1 copy of Foundation Paper Piecing Sampler Block template (see page 115)

Glue pen

Cutting

From Fabric B, cut:
   (2) 2" × 10" rectangles for Sections 4 and 7

From the Background Fabric, cut:
   (4) 2" × 5" rectangles for Sections 2, 3, 5, 8
   (2) 3" × 8" rectangles for Sections 6 and 9

> **Q2Q** I am providing cutting measurements for my foundation paper piecing patterns, as it can be tricky to work out how much fabric to use. Always err on the side of larger cuts, as it's far easier to trim away any excess than to unpick the stitches!

Assembling the Block

1. Place a small dab of glue on the wrong (non-printed) side of the paper in Section 1. Place Fabric A right side up on the wrong side of the paper. Check the position of the rectangle to be sure that the fabric fully covers Section 1 on the paper with at least ¼" of fabric extending beyond the printed lines on all sides of the shape (see the Q2Q below, left). Press down lightly over the glued area to secure the fabric onto the paper.

2. Position a 2" × 5" background rectangle right sides together with Fabric A. Align the raw edges of the fabrics at least ¼" away from the printed line where Sections 1 and 2 meet. Each time a new fabric is added, check that there will be enough of a seam allowance around the entire shape and that it fully covers both ends of the stitching line (in this case, the line between Sections 1 and 2). Pin the fabrics together to prevent them from shifting as you move to your sewing machine.

> **Q2Q** Before sewing, check that the fabric will cover the section and at least ¼" beyond. Hold up the glued unit to a bright light source – an overhead light or nearby window will do the job nicely.

3. Here is where things can get a little tricky. Carefully place the pinned unit from Step 1 under the sewing machine foot with the printed side of the paper facing up. Position the needle a little before one end of the printed line between Sections 1 and 2.

> **Q2Q** This is a little uncomfortable at first since you can't see the fabric as you are sewing, but trust in the process, as the results are pretty magical!

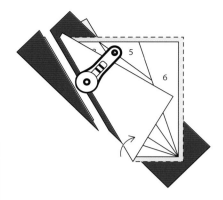

Lower the needle down and then lower the presser foot. As earlier when we practiced machine appliqué, if you have an open acrylic sewing machine foot, it allows you to see the printed sewing lines a lot easier. Secure your stitching by making a couple of stitches, then backstitching to the starting place. Take a deep breath and sew all the way to the other end of the printed line. Backstitch again to secure the end of the seam.

4. Remove the block from the machine and place it fabric-down on your cutting mat. Fold the paper back along the seam you just sewed so that the right sides of the paper are facing and the fold is accurately aligned along the sewn line but not so taut that it stretches the layers. This fold reveals the excess fabric that needs to be trimmed down to a ¼˝ seam allowance. If we didn't remove that fabric, the layers would gradually become really thick and tough to sew through. Using a ruler, place the ¼˝ line along the folded edge of the paper and trim the excess fabric away, leaving an exact ¼˝ seam allowance.

> **Q2Q** Sometimes when you fold back the paper, you reveal a wonky seam or a smaller-than-¼˝ seam. Should you rip it out and try again? My preference is that if it is more than ⅛˝ and the second piece of fabric will still cover the section when pressed in place, I simply trim the first fabric to ¼˝ and move on. The stitch length used for foundation paper piecing is so short, that I'm not concerned about the seam coming undone. A ¼˝ is definitely the goal, so you may prefer to gently remove the stitches, reposition the fabrics and try again. If the fabric doesn't cover the section? Grab the seam ripper. There's no wriggling out of that one!

5. Unfold the paper and finger press the Section 2 fabric open along the sewn line. Press the seam flat using an iron or a **seam roller**.

> **Q2Q** Tools of the trade: I am all about using what you have, but two tools that will help make the foundation paper piecing process a little smoother is a slim ruler with a clear ¼˝ line, and a seam roller.

mini masterpieces

6. Repeat the process from Steps 2-5 for the remaining sections, following the number order on the printed paper, until Sections 1-9 are sewn in place. Position the next fabric, check the alignment, stitch along the printed line, fold the paper back, trim the seam allowance to ¼″, press and repeat.

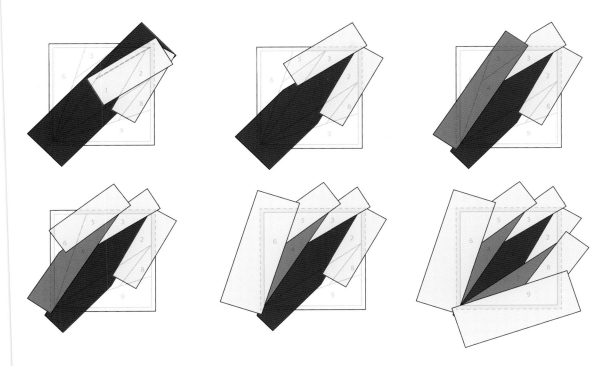

7. Trim the block to 6½″ square by placing the block with the paper side up on a cutting mat. Position the ruler on top, aligning the edge a ¼″ outside the thicker inner line and around the grey seam allowance. Trim away the excess fabric.

8. Gently remove the paper along the sewn seam lines and press the block well.

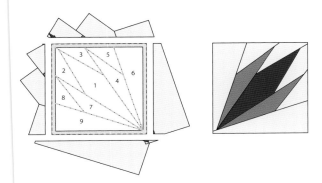

XOXO

FINISHED SIZE: 24″ square

UNFINISHED BLOCK SIZE: 6½″ square

FOCUS TECHNIQUE: Curved Piecing with Foundation Paper Pieced Sections.

I've always been intrigued by the classic pickle dish block and how the emphasis can be on the 'X' shape or the 'O' shape that is formed when four blocks are placed together – it just depends on which way the corner blocks are placed. Why not have both?! This pattern incorporates both foundation paper piecing and curves, this book is *Mini Masterpieces* after all. Let's go out with a bang!

One of my favorite tricks to successful foundation paper piecing, is to use colored pencils or markers to color code the sections to remind me which fabric goes where. I can't tell you how many times this has saved my sanity! Unpicking the tiny stitches in foundation paper pieced seams is frustrating, so color coding plus generous cuts of fabric for each section are lifesavers. That and chocolate.

Materials

For Red Fabric A, Orange Fabric B, Yellow Fabric C, Green Fabric D, Blue Fabric E, Purple Fabric F, and Pink Fabric G: ⅛ yard each

White Fabric H: ½ yard

Background Fabric: ⅔ yard

Backing Fabric: 1 yard

Binding Fabric: ¼ yard

Batting: 28″ square

16 copies each of Patterns A, C and D, and 32 of Pattern B (see pages 116-117)

Glue pen

Cutting

From each of Fabrics A and G, cut:

(1) 1¾″ × WOF strip, subcut into:

(16) 1¾″ squares for sections A1 and A13

From each of Fabrics B-F, cut:

(2) 2″ × WOF strips, subcut into:

(32) 1¾″ × 2″ rectangles for sections A3, A5, A7, A9, A11 and D2, D4, D6, D8, D10

From Fabric H, cut:

(9) 1¾″ × WOF strips, subcut into:

(64) 1½″ × 1¾″ rectangles for sections A2 and A12 and D1 and D11

(128) 1¾″ × 2″ rectangles for sections A4, A6, A8, A10 and D3, D5, D7, D9

COLOR PLAY

Feel free to use the leftover fabric (known as scraps) from your other blocks here. Just remember to keep enough contrast between the prints and the Fabric H segments so that the design is not lost.

From the Background Fabric, cut:

(3) 7½″ × WOF strips, subcut into:

(16) 7½″ squares

From each square, cut two of template B and one of template C

From the Binding Fabric, cut:

(3) 2½″ × WOF strips

Assembling the Blocks

1. Following the foundation paper piecing instructions from the practice block on page 93, foundation paper piece all the arcs using the photocopies of the A and D patterns. Trim, then remove the papers and gently press the assembled arcs. Repeat to create a total of 16 of each arc.

2. Sew a pieced A arc and a template C petal shape together as we did in the Drunkard's Path block on page 59. Be sure to create creases marking the center points, aligning the center creases on each piece and pinning in place before slowly sewing an even ¼˝ seam around the curve. Press the seam to Template C.

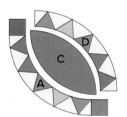 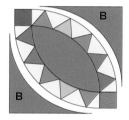

3. Repeat Step 2 to attach the pieced D arc.

4. Repeat Step 2 to attach the two corner Background B units to the assembled unit from Step 3. Press the finished block towards the B units. Repeat to make a total of 16 blocks.

Assembling the Quilt Top

Referencing the Assembly Diagram, arrange the blocks in a 4 × 4 grid and rotate the blocks to create the XOXO arrangement. Sew the blocks into rows and press the seams open. Sew the four rows together and press the seams open again. Give the entire mini one last press.

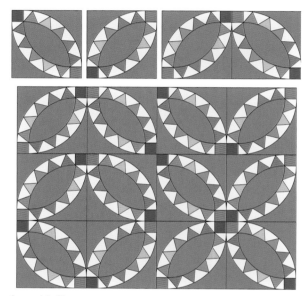

Assembly Diagram

Finishing

Refer to page 14 for finishing instructions on how to baste, quilt and bind your mini quilt. Consider whether or not you want to add a hanging sleeve.

Quilting Suggestions

When you draw a blank on what to quilt, it's always a great time to ask advice from an expert quilter! XOXO is one quilt that I knew needed something special, but I couldn't quite work out what, so I sought the advice of my friend, Erin. She quilted in the piecing seam around the triangles and curves to secure the quilt. Then, within the background space, she quilted approximately ¼″ from the seams and finally filled those in with pointed swirls on the background fabric.

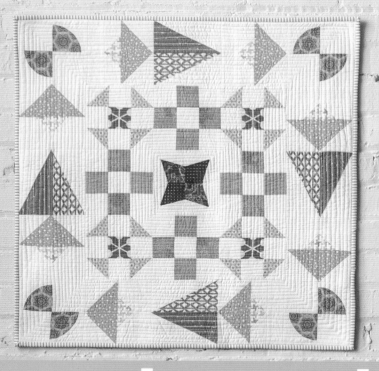

sampler quilts

What's a series of sampler blocks without some suggested finishing options? There are many different ways to sew your practice blocks into a mini, from simply sewing them into a grid layout (below), to adding a background block in between (below, right) or adding borders.

For *Mini Masterpieces*, I've included instructions for a pair of medallion quilts (see pages 102-105) to show off your skills. Medallion quilts feature a block at the center, with multiple borders surrounding it.

If you want to make the a mini combining just the practice blocks you've made without making more, below are some ideas to help you get started. Add in some plain background fabric squares instead of more repeated practice blocks to make the quilt larger. Sewing nine blocks into an 18″ square is the perfect size for a standard cushion insert (see page 17). A row of blocks can be turned into a table runner. Think outside the box for ways to show off your own mini masterpieces!

whirlpool sampler quilt

FINISHED QUILT SIZE: 30˝ square

SAMPLER BLOCKS USED:

- 1 Star English Paper Piecing Block (see page 84)

- (4) 9-Patch Blocks (see page 20)

- 4 HST 9-Patch Blocks (see page 38)

- 4 Double Half-Rectangle Triangle Blocks (see page 52)

- 8 Double Flying Geese Blocks (see page 46)

- 4 Drunkard's Path Blocks (see page 58)

Other Materials

Backing Fabric: 1 yard
Binding Fabric: ⅓ yard
Batting: 34˝ square

Cutting

From the Binding Fabric, cut:
   (4) 2½˝ × WOF strips

Assembling the Quilt Top

1. Make the required number of sampler blocks listed.

2. Referencing the Assembly Diagram, arrange the blocks into a 5 × 5 grid, making sure that the blocks are facing in the correct direction. Sew the blocks into five rows. Press the seams in alternate directions. Sew the five rows together. Press the seams open.

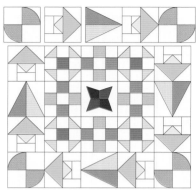

Assembly Diagram

Finishing

Refer to page 14 for finishing instructions on how to baste, quilt and bind your mini quilt. Consider whether or not you want to add a hanging sleeve.

Quilting Suggestions

This mini contains most of the geometric practice blocks, yet still has a swirling effect because of the rotation of the triangle blocks. To reinforce this circular movement, I quilted a square spiral by starting in the center and working my way out. This type of quilting is best achieved by using a walking foot to both evenly feed the quilt through the machine and to use the edge as a guide for your next line of quilting. This is a simple way to ensure accurate spacing between your quilting lines.

ripples sampler quilt

FINISHED SIZE: 30˝ square

SAMPLER BLOCKS USED:

- 1 Teardrop Appliqué Block (see page 76)

- 4 Elongated 9-Patch Blocks (see page 26)

- 4 Foundation Paper Piecing Blocks (see page 92)

- 4 Improv Curve Blocks (see page 70)

- 8 Complex Curve Blocks (see page 64)

- 4 Snowball Blocks (see page 32)

Other Materials

Backing Fabric: 1 yard

Binding Fabric: ⅓ yard

Batting: 34˝ square

Cutting

From the Binding Fabric, cut:

(4) 2½˝ × WOF strips

Assembling the Quilt Top

1. Make the required number of sampler blocks listed.

2. Using the Assembly Diagram as a guide, arrange the blocks into a 5×5 grid, making sure that each of the blocks is facing in the correct orientation. Sew the blocks into five rows. Press the seams in alternate directions. Sew the five rows together. Press the seams open.

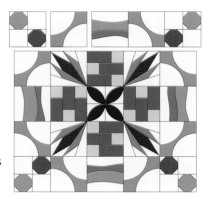

Assembly diagram

Finishing

Refer to page 14 for finishing instructions on how to baste, quilt and bind your mini quilt. Consider whether or not you want to add a hanging sleeve.

Quilting Suggestions

For this mini, I emphasized the curved shapes by quilting a circular spiral from the center out. Just as in the prior sampler, this type of quilting is best achieved by using a walking foot to both evenly feed the quilt through the machine and to use the edge to determine the distance to your next line of quilting.

Acknowledgments

It's times like this when you realize that you'd be terrible at accepting an Oscar or Emmy, because the music would start playing when you had barely just gotten started on your list of people to thank...

I first need to acknowledge Janice Zeller Ryan, who walked alongside me for the long journey to this book. Her time and effort, coaching and encouragement were invaluable. This book would not be what it is today without her.

To Susanne Woods and the Lucky Spool team – when I knew I wanted to write a book, Lucky Spool was number one on my list of publishers. Thank you for making my dreams come true.

I'm forever grateful for the support and generosity of Pfaff for the travel-friendly sewing machine; to Aurifil for the luscious threads that stitched this book together; to AccuQuilt Australia for speeding up my quilting projects with their cutter and dies; to Tales Of Cloth for the accurate, environmentally-friendly EPP papers; and, to Clair's Fabrics for help with the pretty fabrics to make my designs come to life.

Special mentions go to Erin Barry of Quilt By Starlight for the long-arm quilting that she provided on Pendant, Brushstrokes and XOXO and the friendly quilting consulting on other quilts in this book. And to the support and generosity of the other quilters in my life who have listened to my random ramblings at all hours of the day, providing encouragement and honest feedback - Jane, my CMO and extroverted encourager, Alison for her ever-calming presence, studio assistance and the second studio space, and Kate for her unwavering belief in me.

And lastly, to Benjamin, the final author on this paper, for believing in me even when I couldn't. Without his love, faith and partnership in making our family work (and eat), this book would not have been physically possible.

Resources

My favorite tools and supplies
and where to find them.

ACCUQUILT AUSTRALIA
www.accuquilt.com.au

GO! fabric cutter, Flowering
Snowball die, GO! Qubes

AURIFIL
www.aurifil.com

50-weight piecing and quilting
thread, 40-weight quilting
thread

CLAIR'S FABRICS
www.clairsfabrics.com.au

Online and in store; a huge
range of solids and modern
fabrics.

PFAFF
www.pfaff.com

TALES OF CLOTH
www.talesofcloth.com

Accurate and environmentally-
friendly English paper piecing
shapes

Templates

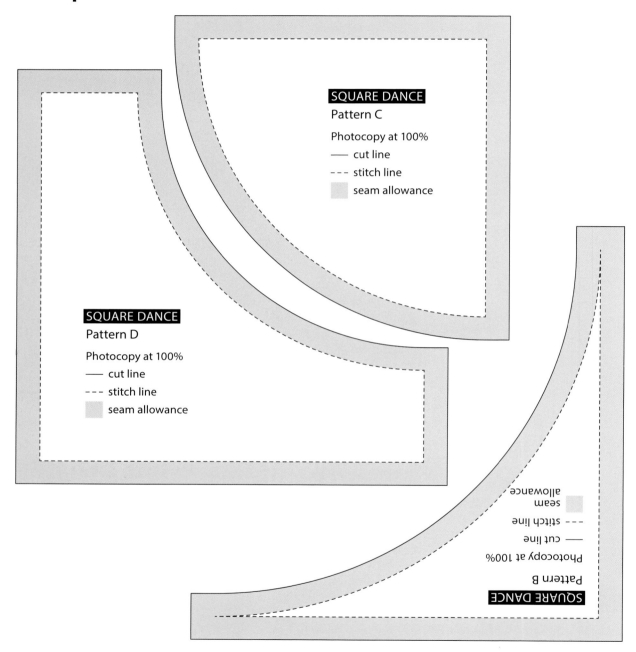

SQUARE DANCE
Pattern C

Photocopy at 100%
—— cut line
--- stitch line
seam allowance

SQUARE DANCE
Pattern D

Photocopy at 100%
—— cut line
--- stitch line
seam allowance

SQUARE DANCE
Pattern B

Photocopy at 100%
—— cut line
--- stitch line
seam allowance

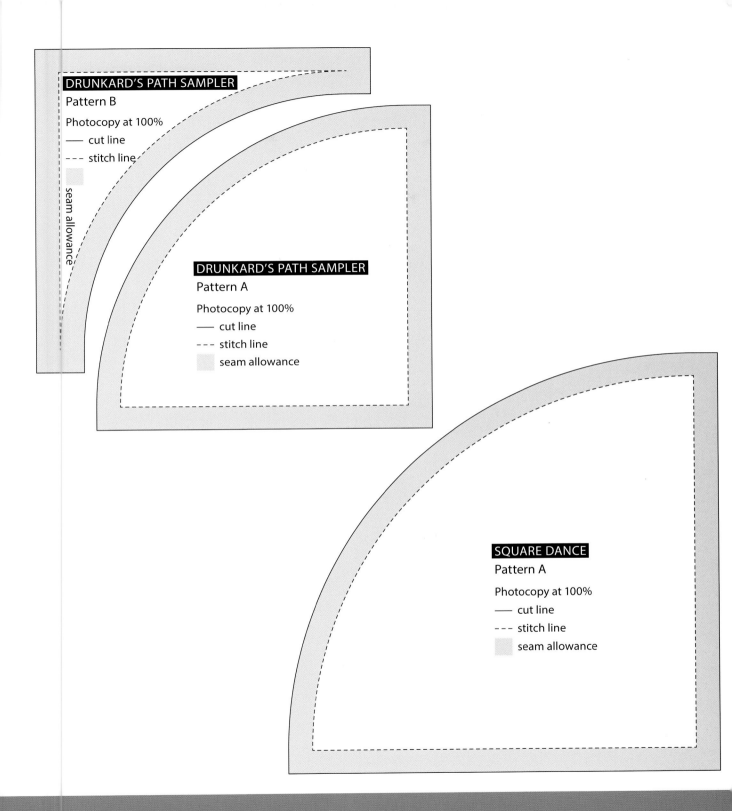

DRUNKARD'S PATH SAMPLER

Pattern B

Photocopy at 100%

— cut line

--- stitch line

seam allowance

DRUNKARD'S PATH SAMPLER

Pattern A

Photocopy at 100%

— cut line

--- stitch line

seam allowance

SQUARE DANCE

Pattern A

Photocopy at 100%

— cut line

--- stitch line

seam allowance

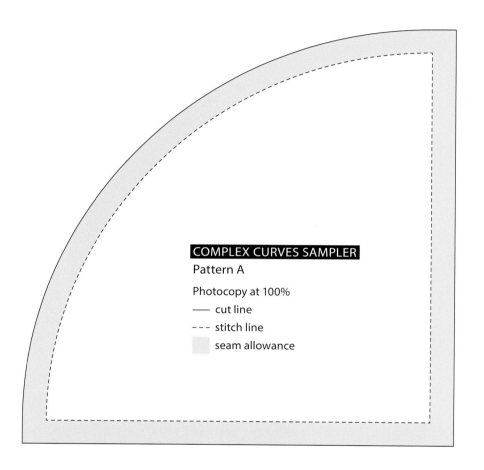

COMPLEX CURVES SAMPLER

Pattern A

Photocopy at 100%

—— cut line

--- stitch line

seam allowance

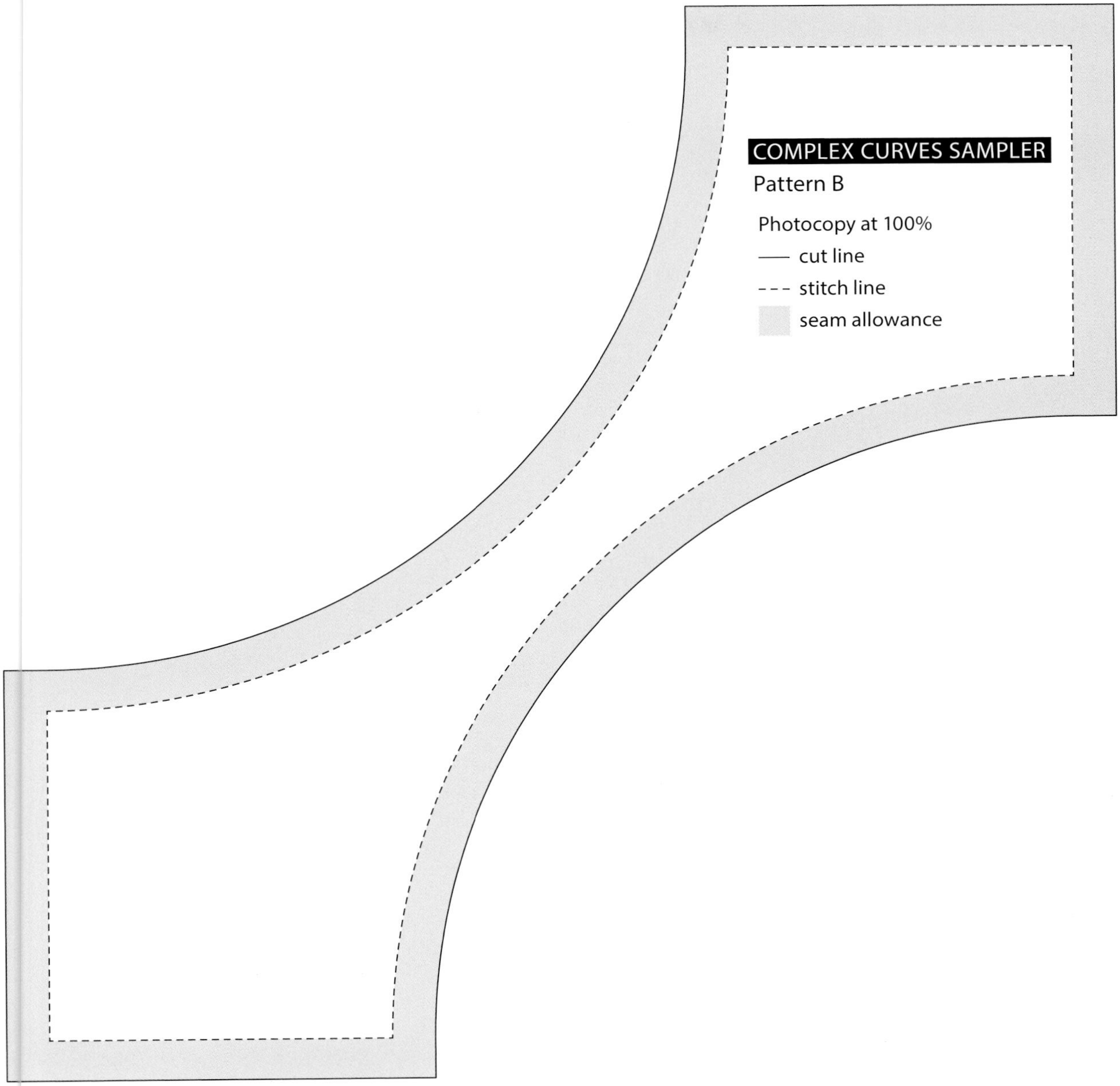

COMPLEX CURVES SAMPLER

Pattern B

Photocopy at 100%

—— cut line

- - - stitch line

seam allowance

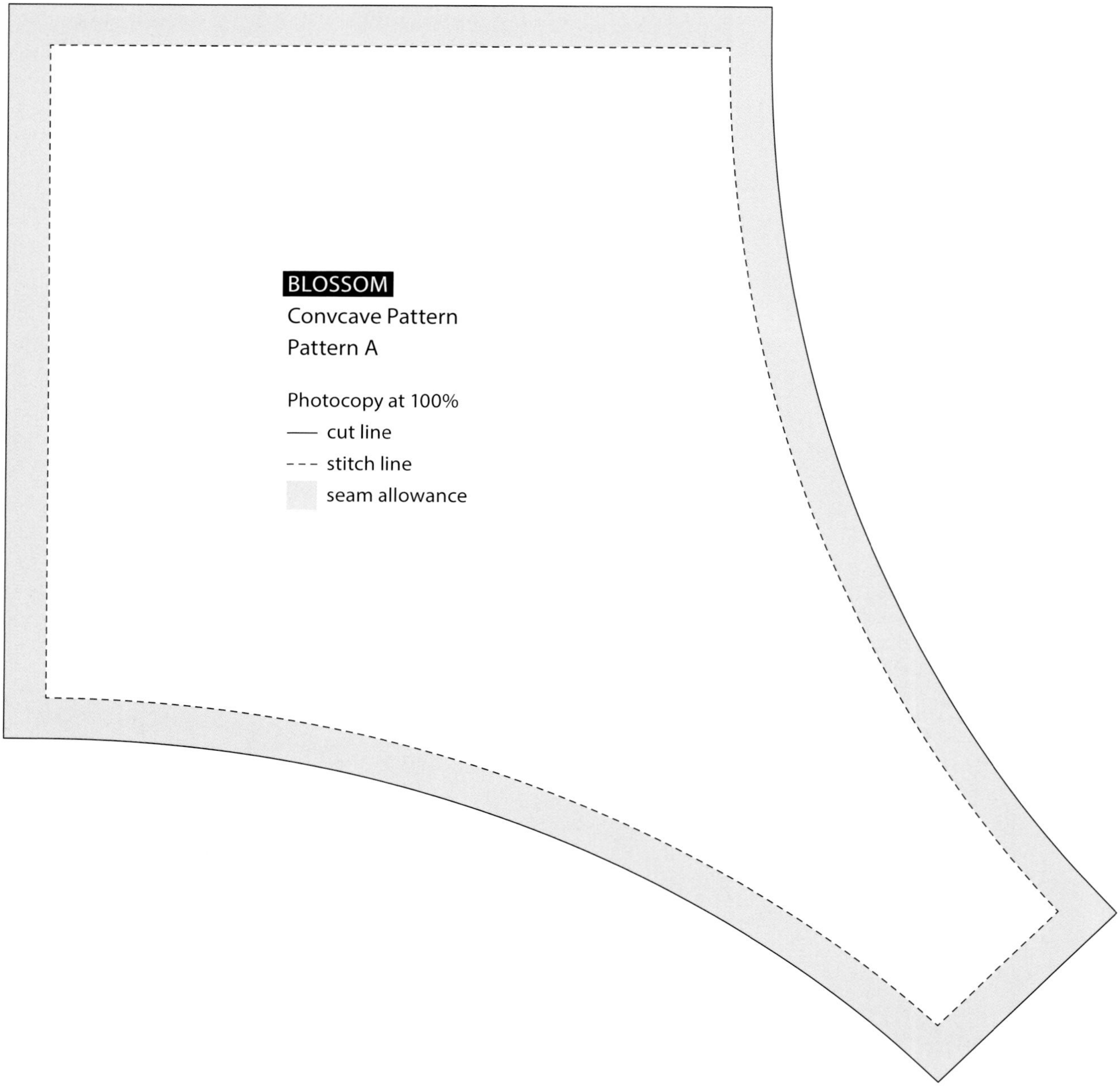

BLOSSOM

Convcave Pattern
Pattern A

Photocopy at 100%
— cut line
- - - stitch line
▨ seam allowance

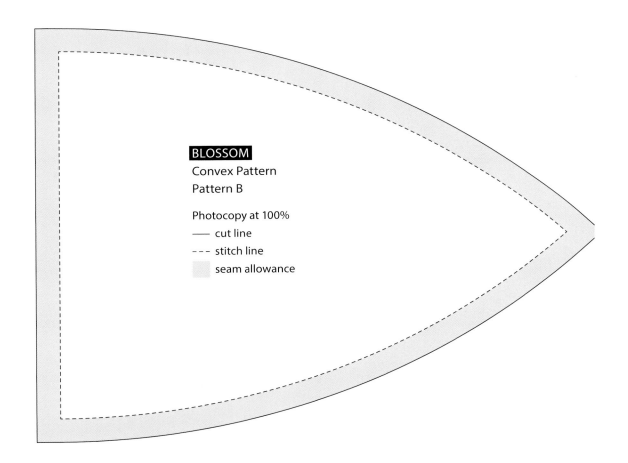

BLOSSOM

Convex Pattern
Pattern B

Photocopy at 100%
—— cut line
- - - stitch line
⬛ seam allowance

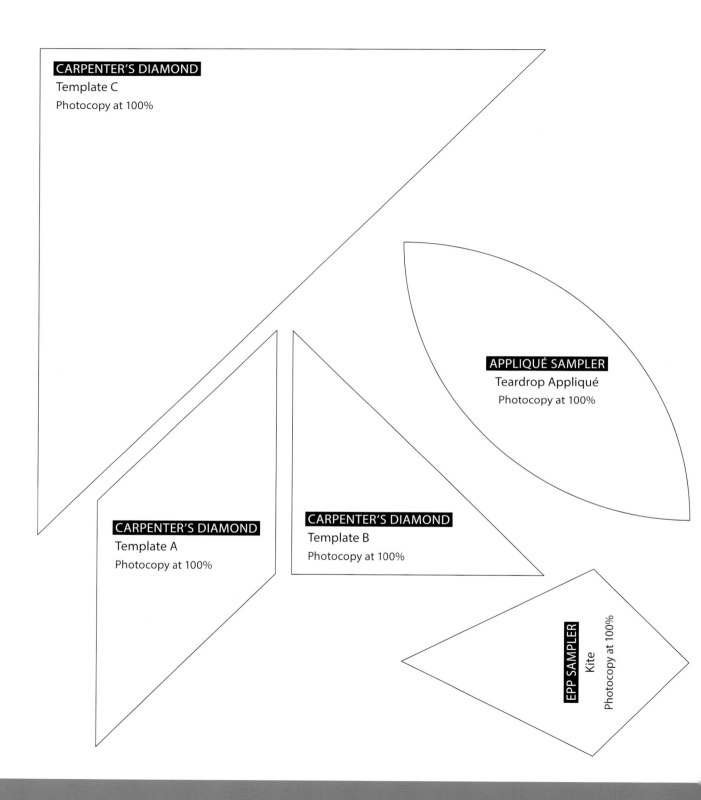

CARPENTER'S DIAMOND
Template C
Photocopy at 100%

APPLIQUÉ SAMPLER
Teardrop Appliqué
Photocopy at 100%

CARPENTER'S DIAMOND
Template A
Photocopy at 100%

CARPENTER'S DIAMOND
Template B
Photocopy at 100%

EPP SAMPLER
Kite
Photocopy at 100%

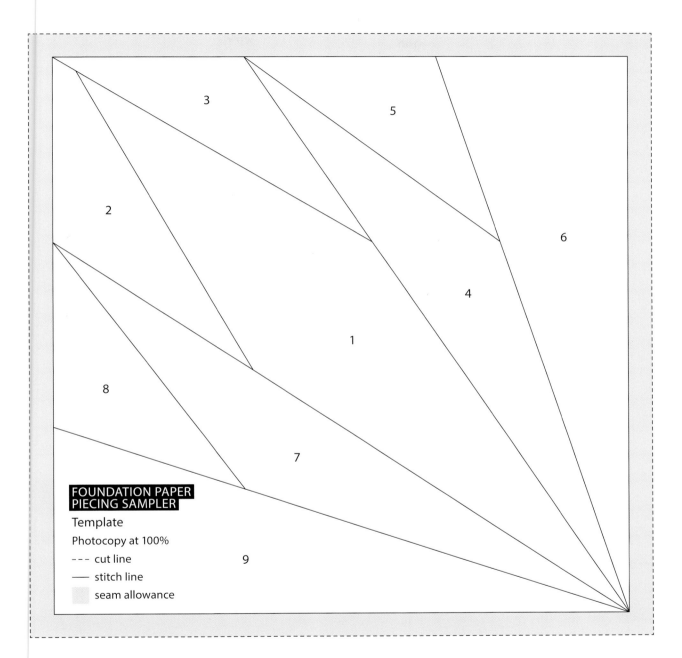

FOUNDATION PAPER
PIECING SAMPLER

Template

Photocopy at 100%

- - - cut line

—— stitch line

seam allowance

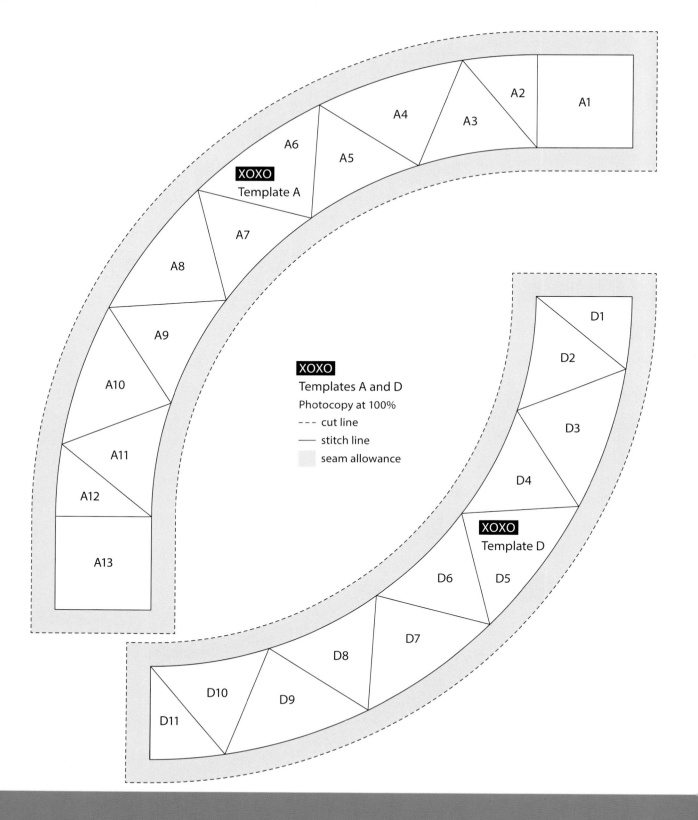

XOXO
Template A

XOXO
Templates A and D
Photocopy at 100%
- - - cut line
—— stitch line
█ seam allowance

XOXO
Template D

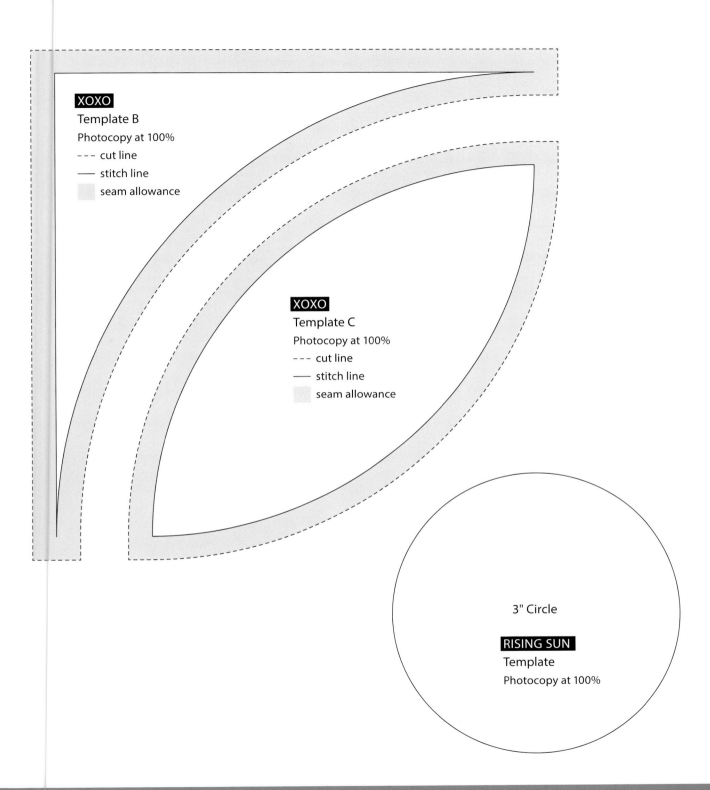

XOXO
Template B
Photocopy at 100%
--- cut line
— stitch line
⬜ seam allowance

XOXO
Template C
Photocopy at 100%
--- cut line
— stitch line
⬜ seam allowance

3" Circle

RISING SUN
Template
Photocopy at 100%

Glossary

BACKSTITCHING The method of locking a seam in place by first sewing a couple of stitches, and then using the backstitch button or lever on your sewing machine to reverse back over those stitches before proceeding along the seam. Doing this prevents the seams from coming apart as you are assembling your block or quilt top.

DOMESTIC SEWING MACHINE A phrase usually used when discussing the quilting of a quilt. Refers to having been quilted at home on the quilter's own sewing machine and not on a professional long arm quilting machine.

FINGER PRESSING The technique of using the heat and pressure from your fingertips to press a seam instead of an iron or a seam roller.

FREE-MOTION QUILTING The technique of quilting using a free-motion quilting foot with the feed dogs of the sewing machine disengaged. This allows the quilt sandwich to be guided through the machine freely, to create quilting designs that often have curves.

HERA MARKER A plastic marking tool used to create temporary creases onto the top of a quilt sandwich. These creases are used as a reference for quilting lines.

POINT-TO-POINT QUILTING A quilting method that often relies on the intersection of seams within the piecing to create repeated designs. A series of markings using a disappearing pen and a ruler can also be used.

QUILTING   While generally used to refer to the entire process of making quilts, it is also the specific term for the process of sewing the three layers of a quilt together by stitching across the quilt top. See page 15 for more information.

SEAM ALLOWANCE   The distance between the cut fabric raw edge and the stitching line. In piecing, a ¼″ seam allowance is usually used.

SEAM ROLLER   A tool often used in paper piecing to prevent many trips between the sewing machine and an ironing station. A small wooden wheel is mounted on a handle and the wheel is used for pressing seams open.

SELVAGE   The finished edge of fabric yardage created during the manufacturing process to prevent unraveling. It also usually includes information about the fabric, including the dots indicating each color used in the design, the name of the fabric line, the designer and the manufacturer.

SQUARE UP   To align the edges of a cut of fabric, block, or quilt top so that it is perfectly rectangular or square. With fabric, this refers to the process of ensuring the pattern of the design aligns perfectly when the selvages are aligned.

YARDAGE   A term that refers to a continuous length of fabric when it is cut from the bolt.